THE BARROWFORD PRESS

≈ POCKET HISTORY SERIES ≈

HIGHER BARROWFORD

ഔഈ

JOHN A CLAYTON

ഔഈ

Published By
BARROWFORD PRESS

Cover design; Barrowford Press

www.barrowfordpress.co.uk

PRINTED IN THE UK

Other Titles by the Same Author

Valley of the Drawn Sword *Early History of Burnley, Pendle and West Craven*   ISBN 978-0-9553821-0-9   2006

The Lancashire Witch Conspiracy (1ST and 2nd editions) *A History of Pendle Forest and the Lancashire Witch Trials*
ISBN 978-0-9553821-2-3 2007

Cotton and Cold Blood *A True Story of Victorian Life and Death in East Lancashire*   ISBN 978-0-9553821-4-7 2008

Admergill with Blacko and Brogden *The History and Archaeology of an Ancient Pennine Estate*
ISBN 978-0-9553821-6-1 2009

Local History Series - **Lower Barrowford** 978-0-9553821-5-4 2009   **Central Barrowford** 978-0-9553821-7-8 2009
(now combined as **Lower and Central Barrowford**)
Higher Barrowford 978-0-9553821-8-5 2010   **Blacko** 978-0-9570043-0-6 2011

The Pendle Witch Fourth Centenary Handbook   *History and Archaeology of a 1612 Landscape*
ISBN 978-0-9553821-9-2 2012

The Other Pendle Witches *The Pendle Witch Trials of 1634*   ISBN 978-0-9570043-2-0   2012

The Annals and Stories of Barrowford *(Republication of Blakey, J. 1929)* ISBN 978-0-9570043-1-3   2013

Burnley and Pendle Archaeology - Part One *Ice Age to the Early Bronze Age*   ISBN 978-0-9570043-3-7   2014

Burnley and Pendle Archaeology - Part Two *Middle Bronze Age to Iron Age*   ISBN 978-0-9570043-3-7   2014

Acknowledgements

Many of the photographs within this book have been supplied by Mr. R J Hayhurst and for these I am grateful. Without the foresight of historians who saw the long-term benefits to our society in the saving of records, both photographic and written, then books such as this would not be possible.

Photographs:

The R. J. Hayhurst Collection
The late Albert Morris Collection
The late Jim Sanderson collection
Roderick Gregg
Nelson Leader
Nelson Library (Local Studies)
Colne Library (Local Studies)
Stanley Graham
Others: J A Clayton

Resources:

Blakey, J. *Annals and Stories of Barrowford* 1929
Doreen Crowther – unpublished papers Nelson Library
Gladys Whittaker – unpublished papers Nelson Library
Farrer's *Clitheroe Court Rolls* Vols I-III Colne Library
Barrowford Almanac series (courtesy of R Gregg)
Lancashire Records Office, Preston
Miller, E. M. J. *A Walk Though Barrowford* 1983
Nelson Leader
Leeds Mercury
Melanie Whitehead (Sutcliffe material)
Pearson, S. *Rural Houses of the Lancashire Pennines* 1985
Published BMD records – Newchurch-in-Pendle and Colne
Shackleton, G. *The Textile Mills of Pendle* 2006
Various deeds, indentures etc. held by the author
Yorkshire Archaeological Society
Mike Rothwell – *Industrial Heritage* 2006
Dennis Green & Doreen Crowther research – *A Bannister Family History* Heritage Trust NW 2006

www.barrowfordpress.co.uk

ISBN 978-0-9553821-8-5

Introduction

The previous titles in this Series, *Lower Barrowford and Central Barrowford (now combined in a single publication),* covered an area extending from Newbridge to the White Bear Inn while the subject of *Higher Barrowford* covers the extended area known as Higherford. Traditionally this area runs from a boundary roughly coterminous with Colne Road northwards to the Blacko boundary but, for the purposes of this book, we begin our historical journey at Halstead Lane, to the north-east of the White Bear Inn.

The district of Higher Barrowford formed an integral part of the medieval township of Barrowford known as Over Barrowford and it is fair to say that here might be seen the first 'modern' settlements within the extended district of Barrowford. Indeed, it is possible that the present day site of Park Hill, which now houses the Pendle Heritage Centre, took the form of a farmstead within the late Anglo-Saxon period (10th century). Archaeological evidence points to this having been a settled site long before the present hall at Park Hill was constructed.

During the 18th and 19th centuries Higher Barrowford became the home of the well-heeled within local society as minor gentry families such as the Grimshaws set up home here. This is probably the reason why Higher Barrowford could only ever boast a single textile mill, whereas the central and lower parts of the township saw a number of mills spring up along the banks of Pendle Water. Higher Barrowford, then, has largely retained its non-industrial air and can be said to contain a higher concentration of buildings of high status than its more industrialised Central and Lower neighbours.

Furthermore, Higher Barrowford encompasses the widely admired beauty spot of the Water Meetings which, as we shall see, has remained largely untouched since the early Iron Age.

The White Bear Inn: 1893

Barrowford Traders etc. – 1834:

Robert Brown – school keeper.
Thomas Haddock – school keeper.

John Blakey – boot & shoe maker.
John Nutter – boot & shoe maker.
John Sharp – boot & shoe maker.
Ambrose Wilkinson – boot & shoe maker.

William England – carpenter.
Thomas Veevers – carpenter, Hubby Causeway

Brightmore & Hudson – cotton manufacturers.
Grimshaw & Bracewell – cotton manufacturers.
Grimshaw & Bracewell – maltsters.
Thomas Armistead – shop keeper
James Baldwin – shopkeeper.
Hartley Brotherton – shop keeper.
Robert Crook – shopkeeper.
Elijah Dugdale – shopkeeper.
Thomas Pollard – shopkeeper.
James Starkie – shopkeeper.
David Stansfield – shopkeeper.

David Stansfield

John Barrowclough – butcher.
John Higgan – butcher.

John Blakey – shuttle maker.
Thomas Ridehalgh – shuttle maker.

Henry Edmondson – blacksmith.
Thomas Whitaker – blacksmith.

Hannah Brown – straw hat maker.
Mary Walton – straw hat maker.

Thomas Dickinson – surgeon.

Robert Buckely (Buckle?) – tailor.
John Steel – tailor.

John Holt – taverner – Cross Gates.
John Hartley – taverner – Fleece Inn.
Benjamin Moore – taverner – George & Dragon.
Robert Hargreaves – taverner – Sparrow Hawk.
Nancy Bracewell – taverner – White Bear.

James Holgate – beer seller.
Jude Robinson – beer seller.
David Stansfield – beer seller, David Street.
William Baldwin – wire worker, Lane Bottom

Traders etc. in 1893:

Alfred Foulds – wheelwright, John Street Works.

Robert Lee - pies, peas, black puddings, tripe etc., 99 Gisburn Road.

Mrs. Riley & Sons – drapers, 102 Gisburn Road.

T. Faraday - cheap grocery store, Halstead Lane.

W. H. Bolton - music lessons, 29 East Bank.

A. Robinson - boots, shoes and clogs, opposite the Fleece Inn.

William Drinkwater - grocer & confectioner, 101 Gisburn Road.

Timothy Duckworth – grocer, 70 Gisburn Road

James Berry - grocer & confectioner, Syke House.

F. Wills - decorator and paperhanger, Gisburn Road.

Henry Berry - grocer & draper, Higherford.

George Laycock – wheelwright, Gisburn Road.

Mrs. Riley & Sons - drapers, 102 Gisburn Road.

Albert Veevers - "Phrenologist and Physiognomist," Park Hill.

James Berry - grocer & confectioner, Syke House.

T. Gard - watchmaker & jeweller, 118 Gisburn Road.

Proctor Brothers - joiners & builders, Newbridge.

Franklands - dress and mantle makers, Gisburn Road.

Samuel Preston - posting establishment and funerals, 8 Maude Street and Waterfalls.

Daniel Nutter – butcher, Gisburn Road.

George Laycock - wheelwright, Gisburn Road.

Mr. Richard Nowell – dentist, near White Bear.

John Kendall - piano sales, 34 Pasture Lane.

Bernard Greenwood – grocer, 106 Gisburn Road.

Robert Crook – grocer, 8 West Hill.

Tom Lowcock - Rossendale, Humber, Swift etc. bicycles, 96 Gisburn Road.

Robert Horsley - chip potato and fried fish shop, 132 Gisburn Road.

Aldersley's Drapers, 102 Gisburn Road.

John Wiseman - joiner & builder, 213 Gisburn Road.

Robert Lee - pies, peas, black puddings, tripe etc; 99 Gisburn Road.

J. Musgrave - cutter and tailor, 143 Gisburn Road.

Mrs. Sharp – gloves, Gisburn Road.

A. Robinson - boots, shoes and cloggs, opposite the Fleece Inn.

Manchester County Bank, Pasture Lane.

John Robinson - wire winder, Hatters Row.

Traders in 1905:

J. Townend & Sons – tailors, opposite the Gaumless Fountain

S. Howarth - Grocer

E. Faraday – stationer, Gisburn Road

G. Barlow – florist - residence 28 Church Street

F. Pate - hairdresser and umbrella maker, 85 Gisburn Road

J. J. Paul - fruiterer, rabbit and potato salesman, 120 & 122 Gisburn Road *(see photograph following page)*

J. W. Buckle - Central Dividend Stores, 98 Gisburn Road

Hargreaves and Haworth - ironmongers (ex Blakeys), Park Gates, Gisburn Road

V.C. Steadman – grocer, 150 Gisburn Road, Higherford

Jonathan Dugdale - grocery and provisions, 12 Halstead Lane

S. Jackson – cycles, 114 Gisburn Road

C. W. Brewster - grocery and provisions, 163 Gisburn Road

Misses Uttley – dressmakers, 79 Gisburn Road

Henry Lord - draper & provisions, 243 Gisburn Road

A. Slater - general broker & furniture dealer, 97a Gisburn Road

John Heaton – ironmonger, Gisburn Road

Corman's (late Stansfield's) - grocers, drapers and milliners, 5 David Street

Jonas Sharp - clogger and boot repairer, 112 Gisburn Road

John Clegg – tobacconist, 159 Gisburn Road

W. Butterfield – grocer, 215 Gisburn Road

J. Seed - watchmaker and jeweller, 97a Gisburn Road

J. J. Paul's cart around 1908.
The horse is as happy to pose for the camera as the delivery lad!

Traders 1905 continued:

Hartley's Toffee Works, 107 Gisburn Road

J. Swinglehurst – chemist & druggist, next to White Bear

N. Pritchard – chimney sweep, 9 Foreside, Higherford

Preston's - carriage proprietors & funeral directors, Central Mews, Nora Street

Joseph Hill – decorator, 63e Gisburn Road

Mark Sharp – engineer & smith, Albert Mills

John Brown – general and farm auctioneer (est. over 80 years), 22 Church Street

Stansfield Roberts – livery stables, George & Dragon, residence 21 Ford Street

Henry Lord – draper & provisions, 243 Gisburn Road

R Barrowclough – teacher of music, 5 Pasture Lane

Thomas Duerden – joiner, builder & funeral director, 3 Joseph Street

John Clegg – tobacconist, 159 Gisburn Road

Oliver Wilkinson – coal dealer & carrier, 81 Garnett Street

Miss S Smith – music teacher, 3 Peter Street

J T Rudman (late Faraday's), Post Office buildings

Badge and Ramsden – plumbers, 102 Gisburn Road

Manchester County Bank, Gisburn Road

Telephone Directory 1905:

Atkinson & Co.	17
C. Atkinson - Willow Bank	17a
John Barrowclough - Oaklands	80
R. Cook & Co.	55
Robert Cook	55a
E. Faraday – Stationer, Gisburn Road	38x1
S. Howarth - Grocer	12x
James Holden - Cotton Manufacturer	1243
John Kenyon – Brewer, Clough Springs	46
Leeds & Liverpool Canal Co.	93
E.T. Preston and S. Preston - Carriage props.	38x3
John Ridehalgh -Oak Bank	32a
Sunfield Man. Co.	207
Urban District Council	74
Vine Spinning Co.	77
John Heaton – Ironmonger, Gisburn Road	38x2
E. Butler - Plasterer	38
Smith Bros. - Corn Millers, Higherford	72
Tom Lowcock – Motor & Cycle Dealer	38yf
John Tosney Ltd. – Albert Mills North	2162

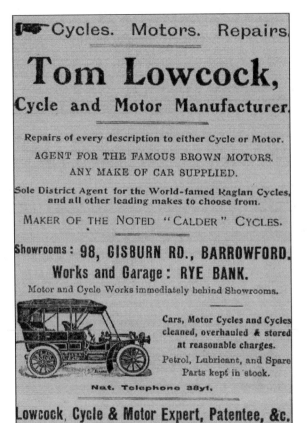

Manufacturers in 1905:
No. of looms

The Sunfield Manufacturing Company - Albert Mills	564
East Bank Manufacturing Company	246
Messrs. R. Cook & Company - Albert Mills	456
James Holden - Park Shed	218
R. Berry & Son - Victoria Mills	1,513
Barritt & West - Calder Vale Shed	264
C. Atkinson & Company - Lower Clough Mills	1,348
E. Wilkinson – Lower Clough	234
John Dixon – Lower Clough	192
Duckworth & Atkinson - Lower Clough	150
Smith & Wiseman - Higherford	480
Smith Bros. Corn Millers - Higherford	

Pasture Lane Mill & Estate Co. – Albert Mills

Albert Mills tenants were:
Vine Spinning Co.Ltd;
East Bank Manufacturing Co. Ltd;
Sunfield Manufacturing Co.
Mr. R. Cook & Co.
Mr. James Holden
Mr. David Sharp & Son

Barrowford Loom & Power Company - Lower Clough Mill

Tenants were:
Messrs. C. Atkinson & Co.
Elihu Wilkinson
Messrs. Duckworth & Atkinson
Mr. John Dixon

Clough Springs Brewery – Owner: John Kenyon of Brymbella, Rawtenstall

Employees were:
Mr. Birchall - traveller
Mr. Barnes - book keeper
Jonas Brown - brewer
Arthur Brown - assistant brewer

Holmefield Mills – Owner: Samuel Holden

John Dixon

Samuel Holden

Clubs 1905:

Barrowford Cycling Club - headquarters at Syke House

Barrowford Conservative Club - president John Holt - vice president J. Kendall - secretary T. Holgate - treasurer J. Kendall - steward T. Holgate - committee: T. Nutter: P. Smith: H. Howarth: J. Hargreaves: E. Hatton: O.D. Metcalfe: H. Lee: J. Buckle: T. Pickover

Barrowford Liberal Club - president Mr. R. H. Wiseman* - vice presidents Thomas Faraday and C. Atkinson - secretary Tom Ridehalgh - treasure John Roberts - steward L.G. Jackson - committee: R. Hargreaves: Paul Sharp: John Barrowclough: James Atkinson: I.W. Atkinson: Robert Skelton: Tom Skinner: David Rudman: Arthur Faraday

Barrowford Co-operative Women's Guild - president Mrs. Morris

Barrowford Angling Association - president W.H. Atkinson - secretary Walter Hargreaves of Belmont Terrace - treasurer W. Rushton - committee: Harry Atkinson: Harry Webber: Charles Hill: Sam Catlow: J.T. Nutter: W. Gallery

Barrowford Ambulance & Nursing Division - treasurer Mr. F. Horsley

R. H. Wiseman: 1892

Schools 1905:

Barrowford Central Council School (Rushton Street)
Newbridge School (infants)
Barrowford National Church of England Voluntary School (St. Thomas's)
Higherford (St. Peter's & St. Paul's)

Traders 1909:

Hartley and Dyson - the Ford Motor & Cycle Depot, 151 Gisburn Road

William Hargreaves - family butcher, 1 Forest View

V. S. Burrows - corn & seed merchants, 81 Gisburn Road

Mrs. W. Butterfield - family grocer, 215 Gisburn Road

Robert Stansfield - John Street joinery works

Miss Nixon – nurse, 166 Gisburn Road, Higherford

William Harrison - shoeing smith, by the waterfall, home 9 The Fold

Mrs. E. Bentley – midwife, Bent House, Spring Lane, Higherford

R. Moore - English & foreign fruiterer, 120 & 122 Gisburn Road

Whitham - confectioners, 5 Maud Street

A. Wells - bespoke tailors, 102 Gisburn Road

(1911) **Holden's** - fried fish and potato saloon, 132 Gisburn Road
(1911) **Dobneys** – dining rooms, hot dinners daily, 143 Gisburn Road
(1911) **Fred Scarborough** - baker, 97c Gisburn Road
(1911) **Helen Haworth** – milliner, 108 Gisburn Road

(Left) **Newspaper advertisement: 1859**

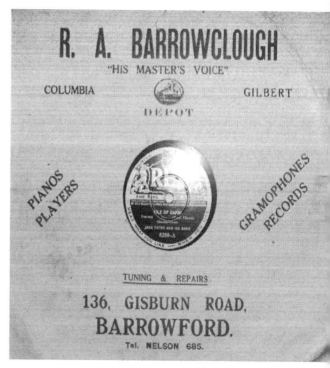

A 78rpm record (Gracie Fields – Isle of Capri) from Barrowclough's music shop – 1934

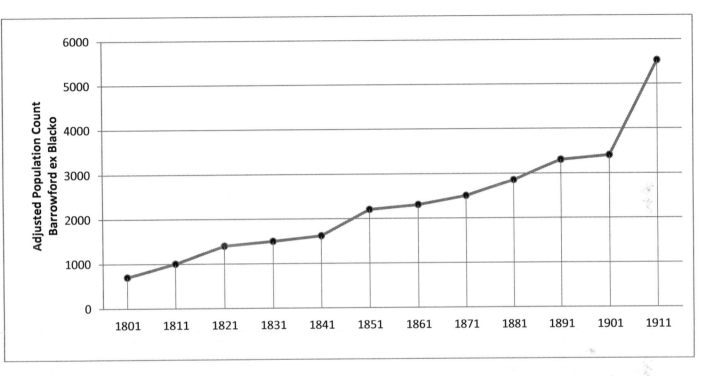

The population chart illustrates the increase in the number of people within the township of Barrowford (without Blacko). It is clear that the population rose steadily over the 19th century but an increase in cotton mill capacity at the end of the century led to a sharp upturn in the supply of basic housing which, in turn, saw the population begin to rise sharply in the first decade of the 20th century.

Taken from a number of directories the above Barrowford trade entries (although by no means comprehensive) serve to illustrate the population growth within Barrowford over the period 1834 to 1905. The expansion of housing within the extended district of Barrowford was a direct consequence of the building of new cotton factories along the length of Pendle Water. The traders of 1834 were catering to the basic needs of what was still a largely home-based workforce who were handloom weaving cotton pieces in their garrets with yarn supplied by the local spinning mills. A handful of boot and shoemakers, butchers and 'shopkeepers' (this term covered a number of shop-based business trades beside groceries) combined with tailors to see to the everyday needs of the people.

In the period between the 1834 and the 1905 Barrowford directories the population had quadrupled and, in response to this, the number of 'basic' shopkeepers (grocers, general provisions etc.) grew by a factor of 300% to 400%. Furthermore, the specific type of trade had also increased; apart from the subsidence suppliers of goods and services the later 19th century, and early 20th century, saw an increase in the purveyors of fancy goods. By 1905 Barrowford could boast at least one jeweller along with decorators, stationers, ironmongers, music teachers, drapers, musical instrument suppliers, plumbers, a bank, motor engineers, cycle sellers, a florist or two and a Post Office.

Not only had the Industrial Revolution now planted its feet firmly within Barrowford but the increase in the flow of the ex-working class people into a relatively new business class was showing itself in an increasing demand for the finer things in life. Fine wines were now available from a retailer at Higherford and the drapers and milliners of the area were able to stock a higher class of stock. The workers, too, were generally better off in regard to their wages when compared to most of the 19th century - although it would be a long time before the heady days of the high weaving wages of the 1780s and 1790s would be re-attained. In fact there is little difference in the spending power of the local weaver today compared to that of their counterparts in the 1790s. The interim, however, told a different story of protracted periods of unemployment, industrial strife and wage reductions for the mill workers.

Halstead Lane where housing and factories sat cheek-by-jowl

The piecemeal growth of housing and factories during the course of the 19th century served its purpose in that the workers were able to live near to the mills in which they worked. People from the outlying districts of the Pendle Forest flocked into Barrowford in search of work and this meant that the already struggling mills in places such as Barley and Roughlee were starved of workers. On top of this, these isolated factories were paying as much for their coal deliveries as the initial cost of the fuel and they could not compete with the Barrowford factories, situated as they were close to the canal and railway stations.

The Barrowford mills benefitted from the lessening of competition as the outlying mills closed and the demand for low cost housing increased incrementally. This meant that the mill owners, who were largely responsible for erecting the worker's houses, were only too willing to make the most of the available land and so houses were built side-by-side with factories, slaughter houses, blacksmiths, tanneries, tripe-boiling works and stables.

Hartley's Garage (151 Gisburn Road) stood at the bottom of Halstead Lane

The building on the left was Tom Holt's clogger's shop during the 1890s and had become Streeting's Cycle Shop by 1911. Within a few years George Hartley had taken the building as a cycle and motor engineers.

Next door at 153 was Fould's butchers shop, 155 was a wood turners before becoming the Barrowford Horticultural and Allotments Society and cottages ran along the back. This was a typical building where dwellings and industry co-existed quite happily until the dawning of an age where public health began to take centre-stage. The lack of private toilets, overflowing ash pits, poor ventilation and cramped conditions, would eventually see the end of buildings such as this. Furthermore, Hartley's garage protruded at an unfortunate angle into the main road and this made it a natural target both for the Council Surveying Department (road widening) and the Public Health Authority – it was demolished around 1932.

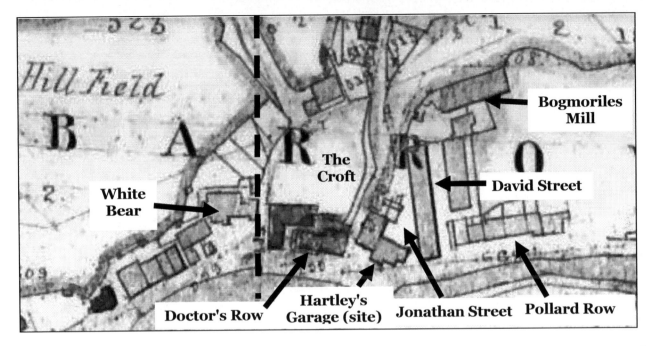

The Halstead Lane area: 1843. The buildings east of the dotted line have disappeared

The growth of industry and related housing tended to concentrate, naturally enough, around the established mills and in the early part of the 19th century these were located at Higherford, Halstead Lane and on what is now Barrowford park. For a number of reasons that part of Higherford above the Geroge and Dragon did not see any particular development of clustered terraces of worker's housing. For one thing, Higherford Mill was not very large and in its early days outside labour was employed to supply woven goods; also, the steep terrain on either side of the river was not suited to large housing development. Perhaps more importantly, though, the Grimshaws who owned the mill, lived nearby and controlled much of the land in the area - they would not have wanted large numbers of their workers living close by. This meant that the building concentrations grew around the Old Mill (in the park) and became known as the Old Row; around the Hill Top and Bank Style area (now Church Street); around the bottom of Halstead Lane and, later, the New Town and Newbridge areas.

In general most of the early to middle 19th century buildings in these areas managed to survive well into the 20th century although some 18th century buildings (such as the thatched cottages below Bank Style) fell by the wayside long before the turn of the 20th century.

Halstead Lane

This photograph is an excellent illustration of the housing and factory clearance at the bottom of Halstead Lane, David Street, Jonathan Street, Pollard Row and Albert Mills in the early 1960s.

The old tram power-line stanchions were still being used for street lighting

Right: Buildings at the bottom of Jonathan Street and David Street

Fortunately the 'Council Offices' building remained untouched

Below: David Street before and during demolition

spare ground (top right of photographs) was the of the Bogmoriles Mill gasometer

Another view of the buildings at the bottom of David Street and Jonathan Street in the later 1930s

The site of the former Hartley's garage can be seen to the left at the end of the houses on Jonathan Street

Jonathan Street looking from Gisburn Road. The row on the left stood behind Hartley's garage

The gables of the bottom row of houses on Halstead Lane and Back David Street can be seen through the gap

Section One of the 1930 Housing Act stipulated that where any Local Authority decided that a property was found to be in such a poor state of repair, or so dangerous as to be unfit for habitation, they had the power to take steps for the clearance of buildings within the area. In October of 1933 the Nelson Borough Council turned their attention to properties in Barrowford and so, in the February of the following year, the Council had determined a clearance area around Hill Top and a hearing was convened under the Clerk, Mr. Armistead, to decide the fate of the buildings there.

Hill Top was the area of Church Street stretching from the frontage of Bank Hall (the Lamb Club) down to Gisburn Road. This included a number of properties, both commercial and domestic; cottages stood to the rear of the Co-op building. A bus-bay and garden now stand opposite to number 106 Gisburn Road and this space was occupied by a toffee works, a tripe boiling works, shops and cottages. A row of cottages also stood at Hill Top and together all these properties were under the scrutiny of the Public Health Committee.

Many Barrowford people were highly suspicious of the Council's motives in wishing to condemn these properties; as far as they were concerned the buildings had served the village well for many years and should be allowed to remain. Witnesses at the public enquiry stated that the buildings were in reasonable repair, were not cramped or damp, there was no particular incidence of disease (other than naturally occurring) and there was, therefore, no requirement to demolish their homes and workplaces.

In his report to the Committee Dr. Markham, Medical Officer for Health, stated that Barrowford had a housing density of 35-40 per acre but that the 19 properties in question (around Hill Top) amounted to 162 properties per acre. In the end it was decided to drop the Co-op buildings from the scheme and to keep the other buildings 'on clearance file.' The end of the properties in the Hill Top area came in a protracted clearance plan beginning in 1936 and ending in the early 1970s. This saw the demolition of the Old Row, Hill Top, Carr Hall, Foulds Street and Victoria House, the bottom of Halstead Lane/David Street/Jonathan Street, properties on Pasture Lane, much of Albert Mills and the Old Barrowford Mill.

The Albert Mills Offices

This building was erected to serve as offices for the mill in 1880 and later became the Barrowford UDC offices.

This picture, taken in the 1930s, shows the ash pits where local people dumped their detritus into the river.

A number of photographs such as this were taken around 1932-36 to illustrate the dilapidated state of certain areas of Barrowford in order to facilitate health improvement.

The opening at river level (bottom far right) drained a stream known as The Clough which ran down the length of Halstead Lane and through Park Shed. The left-hand opening carried the drainage from the office buildings. In order to erect the new mill offices a number of 18th century buildings were demolished including Sutcliffe's Barn and cottages. In the later 1700s this was the site of a smithy, slaughter house and the warping and winding shop where the Berry family began their textile business before building the Victoria Mills lower down the village. The mill lodge which occupied the site of the present car park behind the office building was fed by The Clough.

Gisburn Road and the bottom of Halstead Lane in the 1920s

The Hartley's garage building is still standing. The row of small lock-up shops (extreme right of picture) stood opposite the cottage and shop next to the council offices (above the present bridge to Barrowford park)

Pollard Row: 1920s

The houses on the right were known as Pollard Row after blacksmith John Pollard who owned the land in the early 19th century. Thomas Pollard kept the grocery shop on the far end of the row in the 1830s-40s and was also steward of the Higherford Wesleyan Church.

In 1841 there were 10 cottages housing 30 people on Pollard Row.

The bottom of Halstead Lane to the north of Park Shed

The gables of the large buildings above the terraced row belonged to the Temperance Hall and chapel on Pasture Lane which went the way of many of the other buildings in the area.

The area between the White Bear and David Street was probably the earliest district within the extended Barrowford township to see any serious form of industrial development. Up to the middle of the 19th century this area formed part of Charles Farm upon part of which Hargreaves Great House had been built around 1667 – an entry in the diary of John Shackleton, of Alkincoats and Pasture House, shows this had become the White Bear Inn by 1775. Charles Farm was possibly named after Charles Bannister of Park Hill and stood in what is now the White Bear upper car park. At one time this estate stretched from the George and Dragon to the site of St. Thomas' church and from Lower Fulshaw Farm down to Pendle Water. In 1811 John Bracewell was the occupant of the White Bear along with the buildings of Charles Farm which consisted of; *'a warping and winding shop, 2 barns, 1 stable with a chamber over the top, 1 shippon, 1 pig house, 1 coal house and several closes of land nearby at 9 acres 3 roods 21 perches.'* By 1849 Ann Bracewell was the occupant of the property with 18 acres and 3 roods of land.

The area upon which the Charles Farm buildings stood was known as The Croft – this also contained a mill lodge up to around 1820 and in 1828 the tenancy of The Croft area was sold by Christopher Sutcliffe (stonemason) and Charles Bannister (warper) to John Kitching, a yeoman of Bradford. By 1845 the warping and winding shop, last occupied by John Robinson, had been converted into 3 cottages. Thomas Verity ran a slaughterhouse on the council office site but this was converted into a house and shop by Robert Crook, a grocer of West Hill, in 1836 – the house was occupied by John Hartley in 1849. Part of the former slaughterhouse became a garden area of 251 square yards fronting onto the Marsden to Gisburn turnpike road and it is possible that the present cottages of 145a and 147 Gisburn Road were erected on this plot.

In October 1848 cotton manufacturer John Barrowclough bought The Croft and erected Park Mill there. Living on the site at the time were; James Robinson, Thomas Verity, Thomas Holt, John Manley, Gilbert Higgin, Henry Driver, Mary Watson, Ann Clark, John Farrer, John Holgate, Thomas Dickinson (surgeon), John Blamire, Joseph Blamire and John Nutter. In 1841 streets around this area were; St. John Street, Sutcliffe Row, Pollard Row, School Street, James Street, Sutcliffe Street, Fountain Head, Cloggers Houses, Halstead Lane, Halsteads Farm and Back O' Doctors.

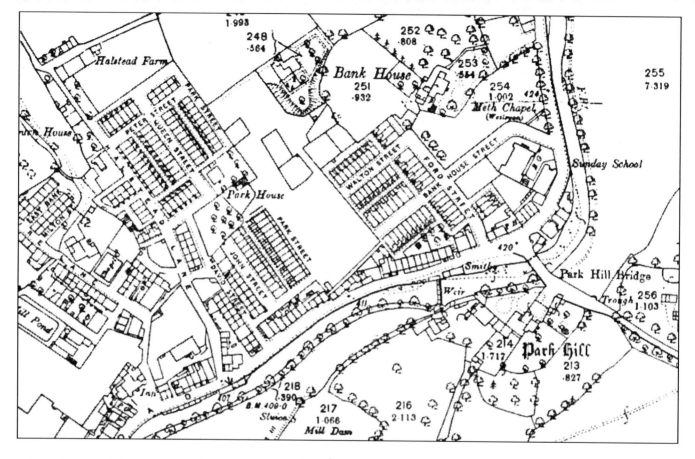

1893 Map: *John Barrowclough's Park Mill has replaced the early buildings between Pasture Lane and Halstead Lane and the old Bogmoriles Mill at the top of David Street has gone. Blocks of terraced houses have now appeared and it would not be long before Bank House Street extended to Park Street.*

Death in the Mill

Albert Mills stood on the hillside on Pasture Lane where the massive southern facade of its spinning department towered uncompromisingly over the White Bear Inn. The first part of the mill had been built by John Barrowclough back in 1852 and his grandson, also John Barrowclough, took over the running of the mill upon the death of his father in 1886. John junior had no real love for the cotton industry and in consequence the mill had not been doing well. In 1892 Albert Mills ceased trading and on Tuesday night, the 13th of September, a meeting of the principal inhabitants of Barrowford was held to consider the steps to be taken to alleviate the great distress in the village caused by the stoppage. It was reported that a great many people had, through the stoppage, an average weekly income of less than one shilling each.

It was resolved to make collections at places of worship and workshops in the township and to invite private subscriptions to a relief fund. On the 26th of October the Liverpool Mercury ran the following paragraph; *'At Barrowford, chiefly owing to the long-continued stoppage of the Albert Mills (which have changed hands), the distress is on the increase. Enforced idleness of a large number of the inhabitants has led to the distress which a local Relief Committee has done, and is doing, its best to meet.'*

The Mercury mentioned the fact that Albert Mills had changed hands and this was indeed the case. John Barrowclough junior had finally sold the mill and the purchaser was James Aitken (1844-1897) of Spring Grove (now Richardson House) at Higher Park Hill. Aitken had made his money through the sale of coal and town gas to the burgeoning domestic and industrial districts of the area. He owned a coal wharf near to his house (on the Leeds and Liverpool canal) and the profits from the black-stuff were such that he had been able to branch out into textile manufacturing. Along with two new partners he saw an opportunity to purchase Albert Mills at a knock-down price with an eye to the fact that when trade picked up again he would be in a good position to take advantage of the upturn – until the next trading crisis at least.

Before his coal and gas operations had really taken off Aitken had run Lower Fulshaw Farm and his neighbour at Pasture was Ellen Sutherland (1826-1856). Ellen was the daughter of Richard Berry (1790-1857) and Nanny Berry (1792-1857) who had built Victoria Mills in Barrowford. Ellen married John Sutherland (1832-1874), a tax collector from Scotland, and the newlyweds lived on Ingham Street. They had a daughter, Martha Ann, in 1855 and before long the family moved to the Berry-owned property of Pasture. James Aitken got along well with his neighbours, so well in fact that he married Martha Ann at Christmas 1873 when she was 18 years old. Eventually James and Martha set up home at Spring Grove and they were soon joined by Martha's mother, Ellen, who had been widowed soon after her daughter's marriage.

Lower Fulshaw Farm

Aitken's new in-laws, the Berrys, were able to advise him on his new textile venture and he and his two partners registered the new firm of West Hill Manufacturing Company Limited with £6,000 raised in £20 shares. The initial partnership contract stated that the firm was to carry on business as; *'Spinners and weavers of cotton, woollen, silk or other fibrous substances and the winding, warping, beaming and sizing of yarn and the dying, bleaching, colouring and printing of any of the aforesaid substances.'*

However, things did not improve in the local cotton industry and November saw over 5,000 looms running on short time in Nelson and Barrowford, with a further 3,000 looms about to close down operations. James Aitken's Albert Mills was weathering the storm to a certain extent but an event was about to unfurl that would have a great impact on his life.

Spring Grove

Early on the day of Tuesday the 27th of December 1892 the engine tenter at Albert Mills rose early from his bed. James Howarth had shaken off the excesses of the short Christmas break and had been in to check his boilers the day before in order to get them settled after their period of idleness. He gulped down yesterday's left-overs of thin porridge, put on his overalls, clogs and jacket and set off for work. The morning was black as pitch as he closed the door of his cottage which stood on the main road to the front of the Old Row Square. He walked along the main road, the clattering of his clogs echoing from the walls of the buildings, and turned up the hill by the White Bear Inn.

The engine house at Albert Mills was a four-storied building attached to the Middle Mill and, to James Howarth, this was the hub of the whole factory; if the engines did not run then the mill did not run. By the time that James' young stoker arrived the engines had been checked and oiled and the boilers were ready to be nurtured into life.

Albert Mills Engine and Boiler House

Manfred Halstead was eighteen years of age and had worked under James Haworth long enough to know his job. He was certainly no expert, he had a long way to go before he could claim to be an 'engine man' but he was, nevertheless, a competent stoker. Manfred lived on Queen Street, a few hundred yards from the mill, with his parents and two younger sisters.

By six o'clock the ringing milltown symphony of a thousand clog-irons told the men in the engine house that the looms would soon be demanding power and Manfred set about stoking the boilers. There were two steam engines of 450hp under James' control and these ran the looms in the two weaving sheds. By half-past six the boilers were up to pressure and James opened the steam valve that started the overhead shafting in the sheds rumbling.

Things went smoothly for a couple of hours and on the upper floor of the engine house James filled his tin mug with strong tea before putting his feet up for ten minutes. No sooner had he done so than young Manfred bounded up the wooden stairs.

"Boiler pressure's droppin' Jim - come and 'ave a look will you?"

"Nay, bloody 'ell lad. They can't 'ave lost much pressure, it's nobbut five minutes since I last looked."

With a sigh of resignation James told his stoker to sit down and not to touch anything as the engines were ticking over nicely. His heavy clogs shook the dust from beneath the stair treads as he clattered noisily down to the boiler house to check the pressure gauges. A few minutes later he had satisfied himself that all was well and climbed back up to give the lad a ticking off for wasting his time - but the lad was not there; James called out but there was no reply. Knowing that Manfred would need to come down the stairs to pass through the boiler house James assumed that the lad was still somewhere within the engine house. He walked around the other side of the engines but he still saw no sign of his stoker until he happened to glance down into the engine crank pit - and what he saw would make his blood run cold until the day he died.

The engine crank-rod powered back and forth within a long trench, or pit, set into the engine house floor. As the massive crank slid backwards and forwards on its never-ending mission small jets of steam escaped from the cylinders and mixed with grease and oil to form that distinctive smell of the steam engine. However, James noticed that there was something else mixing with the steam and oil – the blood and bones of young Manfred Halstead.

As soon as he realised that the lad had fallen into the pit James stopped the engine, this caused the overhead line-shafting connecting the engine with the mill machinery to groan with the onward momentum of a thousand looms. Slowly all of the shafts within the building of the West Shed stopped, and the baffled weavers looked at each other with raised eyebrows. James summoned help from the manager and the shed overlookers, one of whom, seeing the tragic scene, ran from the mill and was not seen for two days. There was very little left intact of the poor lad; every bone in his body had been smashed and the limbs were separated from the torso, in fact the body had been reduced to a bloody pulp. An overlooker, accompanied by the mechanic, went down into the pit and shovelled the sorry remains into a sack – this was then placed in a weft-box, the most suitable container that could be found, and taken to Manfred's parent's home.

Nobody ever knew exactly how Manfred had fallen into the crank-pit that morning. The Coroner was satisfied that all appropriate hand-rails were in place around the engine and the crank-pit had been particularly well protected by rails. Needless to say, the Halstead family were devastated by the loss of a son and brother at such a young age. There is also the consideration that the tragedy affected the new owner of the mill, James Aitken - whether it did or not the events of 27th December 1892 were not to auger well for James.

In the July of 1897 a whirlwind passed over Colne. Richard Storr, a farm worker at Alkincoats Farm, was one of a number of men making hay when the twister passed overhead. The wind sent the worker's caps cartwheeling across the meadow and, as they ran for shelter, they saw their cut grass being whisked into the air and carried away. Half a ton of hay was transported on the wind and James' home at Spring Grove, Higher Park Hill, was at the centre of the fall-out - where the wind had abandoned the scudding hay the house took on the appearance of having been thatched. The farmer at the neighbouring Higher Park Hill Farm, Bill Hargreaves, rushed into his yard and began to rake the unexpected windfall into a stack; this was indeed manna from Heaven and he was not going to let it blow away!

At this time James Aitken's life was totally absorbed into his preaching at the Higherford Wesleyan Chapel but he had not been well of late. He increasingly suffered from depression and as a result he had not slept for a full month. James and his wife, Martha Ann, were sleeping in separate rooms because of his severe insomnia and, on the morning of Monday 9th of August 1897, Martha went into James' room as usual to open the curtains and greet her husband for the new day. The sight that met her eyes stunned Martha and she stood stock-still, shocked and disbelieving. James lay on the bed surrounded by a large pool of congealing blood that had turned the bed sheets a dark shade of crimson - unable to bear his dreadful affliction any longer James had taken his razor and cut his throat. At the age of fifty-three the man whose ministrations had brought comfort to so many had left his widow and six children to grieve their tragic loss. *(Extracted from: Clayton, J. A. Cotton & Cold Blood. Barrowford Press 2008)*

Although John Barrowclough was busy getting his new Park Mill off the ground in 1851 he was still in possession of the tenancy of Bogmoriles Mill higher up the hill. Having little use for the old premises he decided to let his tenancy go and the Sutcliffe family, who built and owned the mill, put the tenancy up for auction at the White Bear on 30th August 1851. The mill was advertised as Lot 1 of a 25 Lot auction where the owners of the land and buildings in the area stretching from Pasture Lane to the George and Dragon were selling land for prospective development to accommodate workers in Park Mill and the soon to be completed Barrowclough spinning operation of Albert Mills.

Details of Bogmoriles were given as: *A power loom and cotton mill with warehouse, yard and garden – now in the occupation of Mr Barrowclough as tenant together with the steam engine, boiler, and upright line-shafting as they now stand. The steam engine is 12hp. Mr Barrowclough holds the mill under a memorandum dated the 7th December 1840 by virtue of which he holds the mill until the 4th May 1854 at a yearly rent of £8:4s:0d. Along with the mill there is a plot of ground adjoining at 1,517 square yards.*

Barrowclough's Park Mill
Before a fire in 1934 reduced it to a single storey. Albert Mills stands behind the White Bear

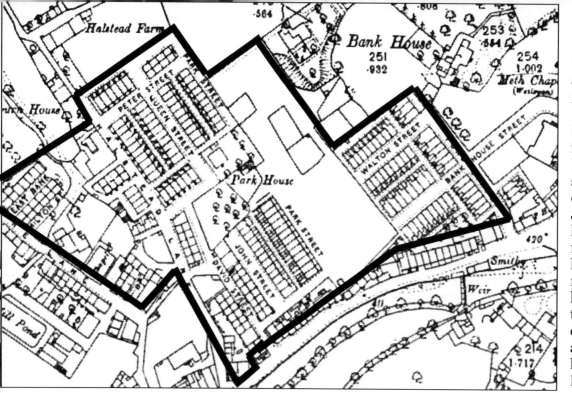

The Area of Land and Property (Lots 1 to 25) sold in 1851

Halstead Lane takes its name from Halstead Farm which stands at the very top of the hill. Although James Halstead and his family were farming here in the late 1790s it would be many years before the lane took the name of the farm. At the time of the 1851 property auction the road was known as Occupation Road.

From Halstead Farm northwards the lane then became known as Oddie Gate and divided into the two farm tracks serving Higher and Lower Ridge Farms - these were once part of the Hargreaves estate, occupied in 1843 by Oddie Sutcliffe, of Bank Hall, and Ingham Walton of Bank House. Oddie Sutcliffe also owned a number of buildings at the bottom of Halstead Lane including one of the old Charles Farm barns, known as Oddie Laithe, and the cottages on Doctor's Row. The Sutcliffe family had probably acquired the land at Charles Farm through ownership of the Park Hill estate.

Other landowners at the time of the 1851 Halstead Lane area sale were John Halstead, John Holt, James Baldwin, Christopher Sutcliffe and Ingham Walton. Lot 15 was described as: *All that plot of building land conveniently situated on the south side of the turnpike road in the centre of the town of Barrowford containing 58 square yards.* This was the small plot later occupied by 136 Gisburn Road, opposite the bottom of Halstead Lane. The older premises on the left were erected by Jonathan Stansfield (builder of Blacko Tower) and his brother in 1853. The 58 square yards of land purchased by the Stansfield brothers in 1851 was too small for any viable building but the brothers ingeniously built out backwards over the river. Jesse Blakey, author of the *Annals of Barrowford,* was born here in 1861 and went on to build the rest of this row of shops before extending the business into Nelson and Burnley.

Blakey's father had opened the original shop in 1853 as a newsagents, hair-dressers, ironmongers and general dealers. By the time Jesse Blakey sold the shop to Hargreaves and Haworth in 1902 the business consisted of a printers, newsagents, laundry agent, ironmongers, oil and paraffin dealers, post-horse hirers, funeral directors and coal merchants. By 1833 the property of 136 Gisburn Road had become R. Barrowclough's newsagency and music shop.

The former Blakey's Shop

The Stansfield brothers (Jonathan and James) who built the first Blakey shops were from a well known Barrowford family. In the early 1800s their grandfather, Dicky Stansfield, was a shoemaker and lived in a building at Dicky Nook which was part of Lane Farm (on the site of Beanfield House). According to Jesse Blakey (*Annals of Barrowford –p307*) Dicky had a son, David Stansfield, who had been a volunteer during the Napoleonic Wars (1799-1815). David completed his five years army service in Ireland and upon his discharge he was taken by ship to Holyhead and paid off with the sum of 6d – he then walked all the way back to Barrowford. He settled down in his native village and bought himself a hand loom, the profits from which he used to purchase a second loom for his fiancé and following their married they worked at the handloom weaving together.

David realised that there was money to be made from the sale of beer and duly opened a beer shop in David Street but he soon tired of this and opened a grocery shop. Four generations of the family ran this shop at 5 David Street until it was taken over by the Carman family in the earlier 20th century.

Mr Carman in the David Street shop founded by David Stansfield

Looking towards Albert Mills from the end of Ford Street c 1930

The chimneys of Park Mill (left) and Albert Mills (smoking) flank the 4 storey engine house of Albert Mills in the distance. Park Mill still stands before the fire of 1934. Behind the cart is the row of Brook Bank built on one of the plots of land auctioned in 1851. Billy Whitaker's smithy stands extreme left.

The George and Dragon

This photograph, taken from a glass negative of around 1874, is nicely constructed with representatives of the social class of gentleman farmer, the landlady (probably Alice Brown) and a businessman with his family. Related to this social grouping we see the three types of transport of cart, trap and carriage.

The George and Dragon was known as Bridge End in a land survey of 1803 and a land sale of 1851 shows *Lot 22* as being the Bridge End Field. This adjoined the inn and fronted the turnpike road (where the Quick Service Garage stands) and covered 1 acre 3 roods and 23 perches. Adjoining Bridge End Field to the south-west was the Horse Pasture (Lot 22) at 1 acre 3 roods and 20 perches in which the roadway of Bankhouse Street had been staked out. Adjacent to this was Lot 23 which was a plot of land taken from The Holme - the field to the north of the highway stretching from David Street to the Horse Pasture. The line of what was to become Bankhouse Street appears to have been a primary land boundary, possibly since the 14th century.

At the south-west end of the Caul Cottages this land fronted the turnpike road and Brook Bank would be built on this. *Lot 24* was a plot of building land in the middle of The Holme and Lot 25 was the plot in the north east of The Holme – this was the future site for the block of houses bounded by Ford Street and Walton Street.

The area around the George and Dragon

Taken from a Bank House estate plan dated 1880

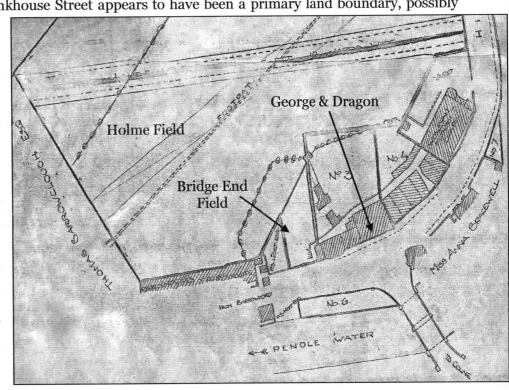

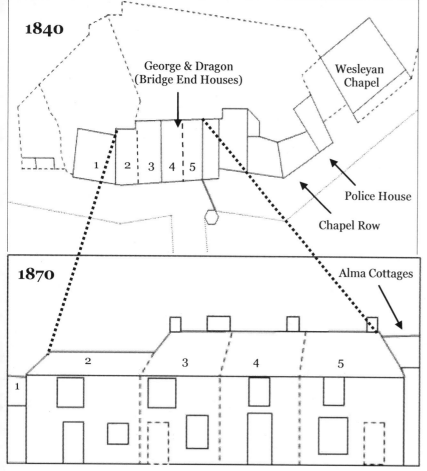

1840

George & Dragon
(Bridge End Houses)

Wesleyan Chapel

1 2 3 4 5

Police House

Chapel Row

1870

Alma Cottages

2 3 4 5

1

George and Dragon: Plan/Elevation

It is difficult to date the building that is now the George and Dragon. Changes in the axis of the building line show that there are at least three phases of construction. The first storey window lintels in the frontage of the main body (4 and 5 on the plan) are at wall-plate level and suggest that two cottages made up this part of the building.

From the front it appears that these two cottages formed a single detached building but a variation in the line of the roof gutter to the rear of the property indicates that the two cottages might have been erected separately. The window and chimney configuration in the 1870s photograph (above) suggests that cottage (3) was not of the same building phase as 4 and 5 but it does align with the single story extension (2).

Bridge End was the name of the area around the George and Dragon from at least the early 19th century and it is possible that the name applied at a much earlier date than this.

A record of 1635 shows that Laurence Hartley lived at Bridge End, within the parish of Colne, and a person of that name was one of the principal copyholders of Lower Barrowford at this time. If this was indeed the same Bridge End as the George and Dragon then it would have been the site of one of the earliest buildings in Barrowford. However, Colne was a large parish and the 1635 reference to Bridge End could have been describing a place of this name at some other site – the area around the bridge at Newbridge (Lower Barrowford) and the 'Roman Bridge' (Higherford) were also known as Bridge End.

One of the earliest records that can be safely related to the George and Dragon is a mortgage document dating to 1763 when Christopher Shackleton, of Stonedge, purchased two properties for the sum of £167. One of these properties was described as; *'Bridge End House which is now, or was lately, occupied as 2 or 3 dwellings and 1 stable thereunto (formerly a shop).* There is a strong likelihood that this is the George and Dragon site as Christopher Shackleton's son, John, appears to have owned the inn in 1774/5.

The three families of Holt, Crabtree and Cockshutt occupied the Bridge End houses as *'possessors, occupiers, tenants or farmers.'* These dwellings would probably have been the cottages 3, 4 and 5 marked on the 1840 plan - the extension (2) was possibly built at the same time as cottage 3 and was described as a former 'shop' – this would have housed a number of handlooms for the use of the weavers in the neighbouring cottage. There must have been a good reason for the shop being turned into a stable by 1763; at this time loom shops were a valuable enterprise. The clue here might be found in the name of Bridge End. The present Barrowford Bridge was erected for the use of the Barrowford to Colne turnpike in the early 19th century and historians have long argued as to whether this was the site of an early ford. In 1875 the Colne Times carried a non-credited article in which a local historian stated that;

Fords in the county were superseded by bridges and one of the earliest on the smaller rivers was erected over Pendle Water on the site of an ancient ford (he describes this as the site of the present Barrowford Bridge). It was a narrow but handsome substantial stone structure, and had a triangular recess for foot passengers to take refuge in, on each side of the centre pier, which was surmounted by a sun-dial. In appearance this bridge was very much like the well known Shaking Bridge over the Conway at Llanrwst which was erected by Inigo Jones in 1634.

In 1749 four worthy Pendle foresters, of the names of Henry Parker, Henry Butterfield, William Robinson and Robert Hartley, renewed the sun-dial in brass but the old bridge was unfortunately washed away one summer afternoon a little over 100 years ago by a flood that followed a heavy thunderstorm which broke over the forest with unprecedented fury, and from the large hailstones which fell in Barrowford the day was named 'Hail Sunday.' The brass sun-dial was found in the debris of the mill pool below by the grandson of Henry Parker, one of the donors who, finding no place for it on the substituted bridge, erected it in front of his own house where it still remains. It has engraven upon the names of the four persons above named, the latitude of Barrowford Bridge, its date, and the quaint motto 'Quid celeries tempore' (the moral of which appears to be 'more haste, less speed').

The Shaking Bridge from an 18th century engraving

It is difficult to find firm evidence for a bridge at Barrowford fitting the above description. That is not to say, of course, that no such river crossing existed. The story of bridges along the Barrowford run of Pendle Water is a litany of lost structures constructed both in wood and stone.

The picturesque 'Old Roman Bridge' further upstream is the most famous of the local bridges and this was often referred to in early records as the 'New Bridge.' Probably constructed within the first half of the 16th century this structure carried the appellation 'New Bridge' for many years and is possibly the one referred to in 1675 when the County of Lancaster ordered an assessment of all the county bridges. Nicholas Towneley and John Parker of Extwistle were appointed as Supervisors in charge of the repair of *'The bridge called New Bridge within Pendle over the river of Pendle.'*

In 1683 the County ordered the repair of *Barrowford Bridge* and this begs the question as to whether this is a reference to the structure on the George and Dragon site. Again, in 1783 the Preston Assizes saw an order made for the repair of *Barrowford Bridge* and by 1815 it is clear that this description was applied to the George and Dragon bridge as jurors were empanelled to *'assess damage and recompense due to Jonathan Swinglehurst for land taken to enlarge Barrowford Bridge'* (Swinglehurst being the

owner of Park Hill). In 1778 a county bridge was erected on the site of the present Higherford Bridge and this was swept away by a flood of 28th December 1837 which also took the bridge at Reedyford. The Higherford Bridge was on the estate of Thomas Grimshaw esquire and repairs were estimated at £100.

The modern Barrowford Bridge

A major piece of evidence within the dating of the site is the fact that the building frontage follows the contours of the modern road and, furthermore, it is place directly at the end of the bridge. This would suggest that the first building here was placed so as to take advantage of traffic. The medieval road through Barrowford ran from the bottom of Back Lane (now Church Street) through the Charles farm site (now the White Bear), along Bankhouse Street (through the Bank House gardens), along the back of Higherford Mill, on to Crowtrees, through the Watermeetings and over to Clitheroe via Colne Gate.

At some stage, possibly following the erection of the first Barrowford Bridge (17th century?) the road began to follow along the Pendle Water embankment and the new bridge, with its attendant increase in traffic, would have made the George and Dragon site an attractive spot on which to build a beer house or inn. This is possibly what we see in the 1635 record where Lawrence Hartley owned Bridge End Houses. Certainly by the middle years of the 18th century there was an increase in traffic through the district as bye-laws were passed to enforce the upkeep of roads by local landowners.

The great majority of traffic at this time was by foot and horse while goods, such as salt, stone, lime and coal, were carried commercially by packhorse teams. Carting of materials by wheeled vehicles was rare before the later 18th century as most of the roads leading out of, and into, villages and towns were impassable to wagons and carts. We have seen that the loom shop of Christopher Shackleton's Bridge End Houses (1763) had recently been transformed into a 'stable' (notably not a barn) and this could well have coincided with the mid-18th century increase in all horse related traffic. If the property here was indeed an inn at this time then a stable would have been a priority. Perhaps, then, the 'Dragon' was a wayside hostelry during the 17th century and became an inn around the middle of the 18th century.

Ownership of the premises has been in various hands over the years. The land was originally within the Park Hill estate before John Cockshutt, of Langroyd in Colne, purchased the site. We have seen that John Shackleton of Pasture House appears to have been the over-tenant of the George and Dragon, at least in the latter part of the 18th century. From the turn of the 19th century it was the turn of the Walton family of Pasture, Ridge Farm and Bank House to own the inn which then fell within the Bank House estate – certainly by 1803 James Walton of Pasture had become the owner of the *'Bridge End public house, brew house and stable etc.'* with William Leeming as his tenant. Twenty years previous to this the landlady had been Betty Cooke, a former servant of the Shackletons at Pasture House.

In 1823 the first row of cottages was built on the road frontage of Bridge End Field (Caul Cottages) and at this time the landlord at the inn was a certain character by the name of Benjamin Moore. In 1820 Moore was one of 4 workhouse inspectors for Barrowford, a position only entrusted to those of some local social standing – this meant that he and his colleagues, Joseph Parkinson, Robert Hartley and Thomas Veevers were expected to visit the houses designated as *'indoor relief houses'* to check the conditions there. The 1841 census returns show that Benjamin Moore, a publican aged 50, lived with his wife Mary (45), son Joseph (7), servant Alice Collinge (30) and servant Sarah Walton (13).

The 'Dragon' c 1936

Probably taken at the time of a road widening scheme. The inn was, by now, a John Smith's tied house

In the 1830s Benjamin Moore lived as the tenant in one of a row of 4 cottages at the bottom of Halstead Lane and by 1845 he was described as the occupier of the George and Dragon Inn (owned by Ingham Walton) rated at £18: 1s: 0d and allowed £0: 15s: 0d for upkeep of the turnpike road. On the 1st of March in that year Moore appeared as the plaintiff in a court case brought against the local mill owner and landowner, Thomas Grimshaw of Beanfield House, Higherford. Moore had a sideline in selling ironmongery and some time earlier he had supplied Grimshaw with 39 dozen pickaxes for use in his coal pits at Foulridge. The tools were valued at £0: 4s: 6d each and the total owing to Moore was in excess of £100. Unfortunately Grimshaw denied that the order had ever been placed or delivered and refused to pay the bill. Moore duly took him to court where he won the case; Grimshaw was ordered to pay the bill and fined £8: 15s: 6d.

In 1849 Benjamin Moore, late victualler and farmer of the George and Dragon, was declared bankrupt and by 1857 the landlord was Stephen Wilson (61) from Horton-in-Ribblesdale. Also with Wilson were his wife Sarah (innkeeper - 47) from Clapham (Yorks) and daughter Sarah (innkeeper - 16) along with Ann Cook (61) a house servant from Gisburn. The 1861 census shows Benjamin Moore's widow, Mary, living down the road in Pollard Row. By 1871 the tenancy had changed hands, the landlord was now Joseph Brown (44) of Barrowford who ran the inn along with his wife Alice (48), also of Barrowford, and their 9 children. Brown was still the landlord in 1879 but by 1881 the new landlady was Katherine Haworth. Between 1897 and 1905 William Haworth ran the inn, in 1914 the landlord was a John Harker; in the 1920s and 1930s Fortescue Hewitson was in residence followed in the 1940s by J. Livesey Cook, Jack Ashton and Jack Blythe to around 1970.

The cottages adjoining the inn were originally known as Chapel Row after the Wesleyan Chapel which stood on the north-western end of the row. William England, a master joiner, lived in Chapel Row and his saw-pit was located on spare land adjacent to Syke House across the road. In 1856 England demolished the old cottages on Chapel Row and rebuilt them to house himself and his extended family — he named the new cottages Alma Cottages after the first Crimean battle of September 1854.

The Bridge End Toll Bar and Syke House

The Toll House was erected in the period 1805 -1807 on the Marsden–Gisburn–Long Preston Turnpike route. This new road had been sanctioned by an Act of Parliament in June 1803 when the Turnpike Trust was formed. The Act stated that; *'The present road is narrow and much out of repair, incommodious and cannot be effectually amended, widened, turned, varied, altered, improved and kept in repair.'*

The Turnpike Trusts were generally made up of investors who were liable to benefit from the massive improvement afforded by the Turnpike Act. Locally there were about 250 such investors including Edward Clayton of Carr hall, James Hargreaves of Great Stone Edge, Thomas Parker of Alkincoats Hall, the Towneleys and Richard Wroe-Walton of Marsden. Below the investors, or shareholders, were those smaller business people who rented the right to take the turnpike tolls for between one to three years and, in turn, these people placed a toll collector in each of the booths, or toll houses, within their district. The toll collectors lived in the toll houses and their wages for collecting the moneys from travellers were invariably subsidised by another occupation such as tailoring or shoe making. Around Barrowford there were toll houses at Reedyford, Bridge End and Blacko with the next onward booths being at Gisburn and Nappa.

The Toll House today

The advantage of the improved roads was that businesses were able to transport their goods more efficiently but this was counteracted by the fact that some local people found it necessary to pass through the toll gates a number of times during the day. The return journey to the Nelson railway station, for example, could necessitate someone from Higherford passing through 4 tolls and this led to an increasing discontentment with the system. Eventually the local people sent a deputation to the local Turnpike trust and the Home Secretary dissolved the Trust on 1st November 1872.

In 1841 and 1851 John West was the toll collector at Bridge End, he was also the village postmaster. In 1861 Benjamin Craven combined his trade as a tailor with collecting from the Barrowford travellers and by 1871 Robert Benson, a shoemaker from Yorkshire, was in residence. In the following year the toll gates were removed and the cast iron pillars were snapped up by local farmers to use as high quality gate posts. Some of these can still be seen at the top of the roadway from the A682 'Blacko Mile' down to Lower Admergill Farm. In the 1880s joiner Thomas England, son of William, was living in what had now become the Toll Bar Cottage and by 1900 the property had become a shop. A tea shop had been added to the rear of the building by 1905 but this was swept away by flood and never rebuilt. From 1923 the premises were owned by William Harrison and his daughter, Ann, occupied and ran the shop.

Barrowford Bridge and the back of the Toll House

Ann Harrison was disabled as a result of contracting polio in childhood but she ran her house and shop, took in shoe repairs and cut hair to maintain her independence. Wartime rationing meant that she had to close the shop but she lived in the Toll House until her death in 1982; the building became part of the Heritage Trust for the North West.

Bank House

In 1474 Robert Bannister was the tenant of Over Barrowford and John Walton had the tenancy of Nether Barrowford; they still held these lands in 1495. By the late 19th century James Walton, a worsted manufacturer, occupied Pasture and Lower Ridge Farm.

Ingham Walton

(1807-1860)

In 1807 James Walton had a son, Ingham Walton (who married into the Grimshaw family) and in 1834 built an industrialist's Regency-style villa on land known as The Bank: naturally enough he named his new house Bank House. Ingham became a local lay preacher and by 1829 he was a leader of the Higherford Wesleyan Methodist Chapel. James Walton donated a plot of land to the Barrowford Methodist movement in the late 18th century and the new chapel (opened in 1801) stood a few yards to the south of the gates leading to Bank House from the turnpike road.

Beside manufacturing and land the Waltons also owned a colliery at Marsden and in March 1853 the Manchester Times ran the following advertisement: *'Mr Walton of Bank House, Barrowford, requires a partner to run a colliery at Marsden – Input required at £3,000.'*

Bank House Plan: 1880

The Bank House estate extended to 40 acres and included around 7½ acres of land upon which stood the cottages in the Fold and Holt Square and all the properties from here fronting the main road, including the George and Dragon. The small building on the plan (right), to the right of the main building (within a kink in the boundary) was erected by Thomas Wiseman as a small chapel named Beulah around 10 years after the death of Ingham Walton. Ingham married Grace, daughter of Thomas and Grace Grimshaw, owners of Higherford Mill; there were no children to this marriage, and the house passed to the Wiseman family (Ingham died 13th July 1860). The site of Bank House was in the middle of what is now the Bank Fold estate and for many years the crumbling building stood silent sentinel, surrounded by modern houses, to a time now past. It is not many years since the old house was finally put out of its misery.

This solitary gatepost stands at the point where the Bank House driveway joined Gisburn Road. The post, and the name of the housing estate, are now the only physical reminders that Bank House once stood here

The 1841 census returns show that Bank House was occupied by Ingham Walton (of independent means) and Grace his wife. Also resident were 3 servants; Jane Oddie, Mary Sharp and James Holt. Grace, now widowed, was still at the house in 1861 when she was described as a land and property owner. The 1871 census records Bank House as number 78 Higherford where Grace (64) was a land and farm owner. With her were 2 servants; Elizabeth Allison (19), from Lincolnshire and James Hoyle (44), the coachman and domestic servant from Colne.

By 1881 Grace had died and, because she had no offspring, the Bank House estate had passed sideways to the family of her great niece who had married a Wiseman. In that year Thomas Wiseman (62 – born in Kettlewell) was the head of the Bank House estate – he was a cotton spinning master employing 90 men, 20 women and 30 boys at his Higherford Mill. Along with Thomas were his wife Sarah (59), son Robert Holt (38 – a clerk for his father), son John (29 – a master brick maker employing 6 men and 1 boy) and daughter Ellen (27).

Grace Walton (1807-1879)

A Tragic Road Accident

The Manchester Times of Saturday 28th July, 1855, carried the following report of a road accident that occurred in the Bank House area:

On Saturday last (21st July), John Hargreaves, Esq. Coroner for the Blackburn Hundred, and a respectable jury, assembled at the Fleece Inn, Barrowford, to inquire into the cause of death of Jane Starkie, a poor woman, deaf and dumb, aged 32, whose death was caused under the circumstances mentioned in the evidence below; concerning whose death Thomas Eastwood, a farmer of Barnoldswick, and John Hartley, of Bracewell, were taken into custody and present at the investigation.

Thomas Nutter, servant of Mr. Nicholas Grimshaw, of Crowtrees, Higherford, said; *'I was standing in the road last Tuesday evening, between nine and ten o' clock, and I saw the deceased, whom I knew. She was deaf and dumb. She was walking towards Lower Barrowford, a little girl had hold of her hand. I saw two men come riding up at the same time in the opposite direction, on horseback, side-by-side. They were at full gallop. The horse nearest to the deceased knocked her down, meeting her right in the face, and she fell on her side. I could not see whether she was trampled upon by the horse or not. Immediately after her fall I ran with another man to help her up, and she could stand on her feet. One side of her head appeared to be much hurt, but it did not appear to bleed much. We took her into William Howarth's house, which was near. Howarth said he would fetch her mother, and I left her in his care, not supposing she was much hurt. She was near the left-hand side, close by the channel. The riders might be about a yard from each other. I might be about thirty yards from her when she fell. The night was rather dark.'*

William Nelson said; *'I live at Catlow, in Marsden, and am a farm labourer. I stood with Thomas Nutter at the time of the accident on the turnpike road leading from Gisburn to Burnley. I knew the deceased very well. She appeared to be about ten or twelve yards from us at the time. The horse on the right-hand side going up knocked her down and ran over her. The horse seemed to falter, or stumble, and then went on again at the same speed, which was full gallop. I thought at the time it was a dangerous speed.'*

Betty Foulds (a neighbour) said; *'I was in the house when the deceased was brought home. I helped to undress her, and I observed a deep cut on the head, and her leg and shoulder were very black. It appeared to me that the horse's feet must have trodden on her head and shoulder after she was knocked down.'* Eleanor Starkie (niece of the deceased) aged eight years, said; *'I was coming down the road on Tuesday night with my aunt, and we met two drunken 'fellies' riding at full gallop, and I pulled my aunt's gown to get her away, but I could not. The big horse knocked her down and the other rode over her. The 'owd felly's' hat was off, he carried it in his hand.'*

Hartley stated, in the course of his evidence, that they had been to a public house, after leaving which at a canter, a dog ran at Eastwood's horse; the horse became unmanageable; Eastwood's attention being taken off he did not see the woman until the accident had occurred. Hartley wanted Eastwood to turn back but he said it was of no use as he had just 'jowled' the woman over, and she would be no worse. Eastwood then said; *'I was endeavouring to drive the dog away by striking it with my whip, and did not see the woman till I was right upon her. I did not know that the horse had touched her at all. I did not know that she had fallen till I looked back after I had gone about twenty yards, and saw something like a woman lying on the road.'*

None of the witnesses had seen or heard the dog. The jury returned a verdict of manslaughter against Eastwood, and he was committed to Preston for trial at the next Lancaster assizes. He is upward of 60. The inquest lasted about seven or eight hours; it excited considerable interest in the village. The deceased was the sister of a deaf and dumb man, who, a few years ago, went by a cheap excursion train from Colne to Liverpool, and was never seen or heard of by any of his friends from that time to the present.

Higherford Wesleyan Chapel

The first Methodist preacher to appear in our neighbourhood was John Nelson, who for a short time assisted the Rev. Benjamin Ingham in preaching, and in forming religious Societies in the villages around Colne in 1742. The first to form Societies, which ultimately became Methodist Societies, was William Darney who seems to have carried on his work chiefly in Rossendale and Pendle Forest. Darney worked alongside 'Mad Billy' Grimshaw, the vicar of Haworth who also preached regularly in Barrowford and of whom John Wesley said; *"A few such as he would make a nation tremble for he carried fire wherever he went."*

William Darney joined with Wesley around 1847 and travelled his message around the country for the next 20 years. In 1878 Darney went into semi-retirement, living at one time in the Old Cottage at Upperhouses in Barley (according to B. Moore in *Methodism in Burnley*, published 1899) – this area having been one of his favourite places to preach on account of the willingness of the local people to take Methodism into their lives. Every week Darney walked to nearby Windy Harbour Farm to buy a pound of butter at 3d. He had now become *'a feeble, white-haired old man'* and died in 1774. Darney's adventures within his preaching life were legendary and he was not forgotten by his contemporaries.

Old Upperhouses Cottage

Like most of the early Methodist preachers Darney met with great and sometimes violent opposition, and once at least he was imprisoned. When he first attempted to preach at Padiham the vicar and his companions attacked him and drove him away. He was frequently dragged through the river, and otherwise abused by the mobs that gathered in the neighbourhood of Colne. Near Accrington he was treated with the greatest indignity by being thrown into the River Hyndburn; as an encore one of the crowd defecated in his wig. At Yeadon a mob led by the curate of Guiseley threw eggs in his face as he was preaching, dragged him down and stamped on him. At Almondbury he was knocked down, pulled by the hair, and almost killed by a mob of people who kicked him with their clogs.

In Barrowford it is believed that Methodist meetings were taking place at least by 1779 when James Ridehalgh, a farmer at Park Hill, entertained regular groups of like-minded brethren. Prayer meetings were held at the Old Row for some time before Barrowford was placed on the Methodist Circuit Plan. Preaching services were also held at the house of Dolly Isherwood, who kept a grocers shop at Higherford, and two other early leaders were John Tattersall and John Wilkinson.

The best recorded illustrations of the ill-feeling shown towards the travelling preachers are those relating to the visits made to the area by John Wesley (1703-1791). Wesley is said to have preached at Clough (Clough Farm stood opposite the new St. Thomas' church) in 1774 and 1776 at which time he stayed at West Pasture. He recorded his second visit to the area on the 25th August, 1748, in his diary;

I rode with Mr. Grimshaw to Roughlee where T. Colbeck, of Keighley, was to meet us. We were stopped again and again, and begged not to go on, for a large mob from Colne was gone before us. Coming a little farther, we understood that they had not yet reached Roughlee. So we hastened on that we might be there before them. All was quiet when we came. I was a little afraid for Mr. Grimshaw, (who up to this time does not seem to have met with any violent opposition) but it needed not; he was ready to go to prison or to death for Christ's sake. At half-hour after twelve I began to preach. I had about half finished my discourse when the mob came pouring down the hill like a torrent. After exchanging a few words with their captain, to prevent any contest, I went with him as he required.

When we came to Barrowford, two miles off, the whole army drew up in battle-array before the house into which I was carried, with two or three of my friends (this house is supposed to have been the White Bear). After I had been detained above an hour, their captain went out and I followed him, and desired him to conduct me whence I came.

Wesley made his escape but, many of his followers having been badly beaten by the mob, he wrote to the Rev. White of Colne complaining bitterly about this incident. White was held responsible for many of the occasions where large groups of his followers attacked itinerant preachers; whenever he got wind of a visit by one Methodist or other he would assemble a few ring-leaders at the Colne market cross and pay them a shilling each, along with free ale, to stir up the rougher local element to disrupt the preaching meetings. These ugly incidents have often been held up by social reformers as an illustration of the wild nature of the working people around the Colne district at that time.

This, of course, is an over simplification of the matter. It has to be remembered that the incumbents of the established church depended on a variety of sources for their income.

__The 'Stone Brigg' area of Roughlee__ — said to have been the scene of the attack upon John Wesley and his followers in 1748

Not least amongst the stream of income enjoyed by the 18th century clergy were marriage, Christening and burial services. The higher the attendant congregation within the parish and the more paying 'customers' the vicar had. However, the rapid growth of non-conformism had long been a thorn in the side of the conventional church, especially since the Civil War, and it was viewed as a severe threat to both the power-base and the income of the Establishment. Consequently the loyal churchgoing people were often subjected to an increasingly vociferous anti-Methodist litany by the parish incumbent - this played on the simple man and woman's fear of any new influence upon their lives.

It has to be said that the rising non-conformist movements were also centred upon power; it was the aim of the preachers to convert as many people as possible to their cause and thereby make a name for themselves. It was common for two services to be held each day during the summer where two preachers would vie for the souls of their congregation – the evening preacher would often berate the preacher who had taken the morning service and attempt to outdo his opposite number with sermons of fire and brimstone. Before the establishment of chapels within Barrowford meetings were usually held outdoors in summer – Blacko Hillside and the Watermeetings being popular sites. Another favourite meeting place during the latter half of the 18th century was the barn at Park Hill where it is recorded that some summer evening meetings were so well attended that the congregation spilled out into the farm yard and even into the neighbouring fields.

Benjamin Ingham, who founded the Inghamite movement, preached at Barrowford in 1761 and is said to have stood on the 'Coach Stone' to deliver his message to the mass of people who turned out to hear him.

Entertainment was very limited at this time and the appearance of a celebrity preacher was akin to a concert by one of today's pop stars. Furthermore, society was entering a new industrial age; men such as Arkwright were forging the future in their workshops and people were gathering within growing conurbations around the new factories.

The Water Meetings 'Coach Stone' The upper surface of this massive stone is level and formed an ideal platform for early travelling preachers. The stone was formerly accompanied by a smaller stone until this latter was washed away by flood. The two were formerly known as the 'Coach and Four'

The Wesleyan Sunday School
Erected by public prescription in 1834. By 1880 there were 250 scholars on the school books

Chapels became a focal point for social meetings and business dealings. On top of this guilt was 'all in fashion' and the firebrand sermons of the performing preachers were touching a nerve within the new manufacturing class who were making unprecedented sums of money from the labours of their workforce. Those mill owners who possessed a social conscience, and had time enough on their hands to contemplate their perceived sins, found that the chapel provided a salve for any guilt they may have carried.

As we have seen, the Higherford Wesleyan Methodist chapel was built in 1800 on land donated by James Walton and opened in 1801. The chapel was enlarged in 1813 and during the building work services were held in a barn on the Walton estate – this could well have been the barn on the southern end of the row of cottages standing next to what was the Bank House entrance (below The Fold). In 1814 the enlarged Higherford chapel was formally opened by the Rev. Richard Watson and a new trust was formed, composed of the following: *John Watson, Henry Myers, Thomas Wilkinson, James Hartley, John Kaye, James Ayrton, Nathan Pickles, William Corlass, Thomas Corlass, Thomas Grimshaw, John Holt, James Clegg, C. Grimshaw, William Varley, Abraham Robinson, Robert Watson, and Jonas Lee.* Most of the leaders of the newly established chapels in the early 19th century were business people and those of a high social standing – this is reflected in the above list of leaders and in the following list for

1829: *Ingham Walton, James Clegg, Thomas Corlass (owner of Reedyford Mill and builder of Corlass Street), William England (master joiner - died 1853/4), Christopher Grimshaw (owner of Higherford Mill) and, in 1831, James Dugdale (a local farmer).*

Thomas Pollard was the Wesleyan Chapel Steward in 1845, Thomas Hargreaves in 1846, Thomas Wiseman (who built his own small chapel – Beulah – in the grounds of Bank House) was assistant Steward in 1846 and James Stansfield was appointed Leader in 1854. William Towler was Steward in 1854 along with Henry Nuttall and Robert Blakey (grandfather of Jesse Blakey). In 1855 Richard Brown (tea dealer and piano tuner who lived opposite the caul, below the George and Dragon) was a member of the Chapel along with Francis Helm who went on to start an iron foundry in Padiham.

In 1881 Thomas Wiseman of Bank House promised a site for a new Wesleyan Chapel (valued at £1,600), adjacent to the old one, and his son, Robert Holt Wiseman duly fulfilled his father's promise in 1888. The new chapel was opened in January 1890 and the old chapel became the Sunday school until it was demolished in 1959. In 1990 the second chapel was demolished and a third chapel built on the site. The second chapel was rebuilt in the Japanese city of Hachioji where it was renamed the Grand Victoria Chapel and used as a wedding venue.

Higherford United FC 1808-1809
Probably the Wesleyan chapel team

Barrowford's last working blacksmith
Bill Whitaker in the 1950s

Bill Whitaker's smithy stood on what is now a plot of spare ground below the bridge opposite the George and Dragon. This building was originally erected to serve as stables, possibly for the George and Dragon or for the use of a local carting firm. Indeed, by the last quarter of the 19th century the building was the stables for Samuel Preston, *'Carriage Proprietor and Funeral Undertaker'* who gave his address as *"Waterfalls" – near the George and Dragon.'*

It is difficult to say when the stables were converted to a smith's shop but this had taken place by the early 19th century. Bill Whitaker was the last working smith in Barrowford; over the past two centuries there had been a number of smithies in the village but the gradual demise of horse-drawn transport saw the traditional trade dwindle. Over the period 1910 - 1960 the horse related work dried up – the old blacksmith's trade had now changed to that of machine engineer and auto mechanic.

Samuel Preston,
Carriage Proprietor and Funeral Undertaker,

Bill Whitaker ceased to trade in the 1960s but outside his abandoned smithy a massive pile of rusting discarded horseshoes stood silent sentinel to times long gone by. The building was demolished under a road-widening scheme of the early 1960s. Around 30 years ago my late uncle, Albert Morris, wrote an article on Bill Whitaker from which the following is extracted:

I knew Bill Whitaker and his wife quite well when I lived in Bankhouse Street, the row next to Bill's in Ford Street, Barrowford. The front door of his home was across the street from the George and Dragon Inn. Although he originated in Silsden, Yorkshire, Bill lived most of his life in Barrowford. He kept in constant contact with his home county having a 'get-away-from-it-all' weekend hut at Cracoe, near Skipton.

The Smithy in the 1930s

Dick Bolton, the well known Barrowford plumber who lived across the road from Bill's smithy, and was one of Bill's pals, also had a weekend hut at Stainforth, near Settle. He and Bill often took the children of both families, and various friends, on their motorcycle combinations, a popular mode of travel of the day, while some of us, friends of their children, pedalled our cycles on the journey to one or other of the places. A tent was pitched for the men and boys while the girls shared the luxury and privacy of the hut.

Bill was an easy-going and friendly person who never seemed to have a care in the world, loving his work and highly thought of by his customers and the people who knew him. His smithy was in Gisburn Road, a few strides from his home, and was an old single story building which had on its front apex a finial with a ball on top and a big sliding door across the front. It was built close to the waterfall, across from the present day petrol station.

*A*fter school, we would watch him at his work. He always wore a thick leather apron and, sitting on a stool, he would take a horse's leg and after bending it would lift the leg onto his knee, pulling out the nails of the worn-out shoe with a big pair of pincers. After removing the shoe he would than pare off the overgrowth, press a new red-hot shoe onto the hoof, 'turn it in' to a snug fit and then quench the glowing iron before nailing it in place.

A small door in the smithy opened at the riverside providing access to a stile in the river wall with two stone steps, the bottom one being near the water level where Bill could collect water in a bucket to top

Two steps from smithy down to water level

Stone marking original height of waterfall

up his horseshoe quenching water trough – the smithy had no town water supply. The steps are still there and have had people over the years wondering what their use was, as the stile appears to have been built for access to a non-existent path across the top of the waterfall to the park. Here the 'take-off' water from the top of the waterfall, or caul, runs into a watercourse supplying the park lake. This was originally the mill dam which supplied water to power the water wheel in the old mill (now long gone) at the far end of the park.

*A*fter retiring, his wife having died, Bill 'took his home up' as they used to say, selling all his household effects before going to live with his daughter. At this time I bought from him a set of drawers for use in my workshop, paying him the nominal sum of £1 that he had asked for them. I used the drawers for years and *one day, long after Bill had died, I decided to clean out the drawers. After turning them over one by one, I found an old £1 note pinned to the underside of one of them. Who had pinned the note there, and why, remains a mystery as I was never able to ask Bill. With the demolition of Bill's defunct smithy in the 1960s all traces of the building vanished and Billy Blacksmith went into history, remembered only by the 'older end.'*

Born William Henry Whitaker in 1881 Bill had been a tee-totaller all of his life although this did not prevent him from serving as the President of the Rouse Club in Nelson. Bill was a fan of the poet Robert Burns and was fond of quoting him chapter and verse whenever the opportunity arose. He was also a keen sports fan, he followed Burnley Football Club throughout all the seasons that he had lived in Barrowford – by 1960 he had seen most of the club's matches (home and away) over a period of 48 years. He had also been a member of Nelson Cricket Club for many years.

Bill was also a keen motorcyclist and recalled that early in his long motorcycling career he had paid the princely sum of £65 for a machine only to see his pride and joy go up in flames the same afternoon when a friend carelessly tossed away a cigarette! During the very early years of the 20th century Bill set off to York races on a newly acquired machine and managed the journey in less than two hours. Unfortunately the bike would not start when he was ready to return home and it took him two days to push the machine from York to Crosshills. Stopping at the latter place for a breather he casually moved the advance/retard lever and gave the engine a turn – needless to say it started first kick and he was home within fifteen minutes!

Bill with a Customer

Cottages on Gisburn Road: Left: 235   Above: 239-247

Returning to the former Bank House estate we find above the Higherford Wesleyan Chapel a cluster of dwellings stretching alongside the main road. Next to the first roadside cottage is a barn dating to the later 17th century; this was probably one of the agricultural buildings attached to the nearby farm which became Holt Square. This row, numbering 231-237 Gisburn Road, were built around 1830; 233 to 237 were formerly back to back. Number 233 was built on the site of an earlier building on the site of 231 and numbers 237-237 were built alongside. The row higher up (239-247) were built as weaver's cottages, 239 being the last cottage to be built. 245 and 247 were the first in the row and date to around the 1780s. Two of the cottages have four-light windows on the first floor to maximise light for the handloom weavers; 239 has a three-light stepped 'Pennine' window on the ground floor and dates c 1820-1830.

Holt Square

Holt Square is often taken to be a row of cottages and it has indeed been occupied as such for many years. However, the building was originally a house of relatively high status consisting of a central hall flanked on either end by plain wings. Looking at the photograph above the left wing was a parlour and the right wing formed a service area. A central entrance way led on to a through passage in the main hall from which each wing could be accessed. It is likley that the original building was erected sometime between 1580 and 1600 by a wealthy local yeoman. The building possibly ceased to be used for farming during the first part of the 18th century and the type of door casements used to convert two of the windows into new entrances suggest that by around 1850 the building was occupied as four separate dwellings. In 1841 the two families of Smith and Holt were residing here.

The Fold and Holt Square

The Fold adjoins with the east gable of Holt Square and consists of three cottages dating to the final quarter of the 18th century. The shed in the foreground of the photograph occupies the site of the lock-up used by the 19th century local constabulary to house miscreants for the night.

The census returns of 1841 to 1881 show that there were 119 individuals living in the Fold (then called 'Butterfield Fold'), Holt Square (then 'Holts') and the main road cottages down to the George and Dragon. Taking this into account we have around 20 separate dwellings with 21 families averaging 6 people within each household. The surnames of the occupiers of this area in 1841 were; *Clegg, Greenhow, England, Friar, Wilkinson, Foulds, Baldwin, Nuttall, Ridehalgh, Walton, Hacking, Hatton, Stansfield, Blakey, Bracewell, Varley, Butterfield, Holmes, Atkinson, Silverwood, Smith, Holt and Sellers.*

The average number here of 6 per family does not reflect the general trend at that time for large families of both handloom and powerloom weavers to live in cramped conditions where any room (cellars and attics included)would be converted to living space. The reason why Barrowford did not see the overcrowded slum conditions of the more populated cotton districts was partly because only a limited number of new spinning and weaving factories existed here. Also, they were founded at staggered time intervals and this meant that house building for the incoming workers was able to keep pace.

Leeds Mercury Ad: January 1861

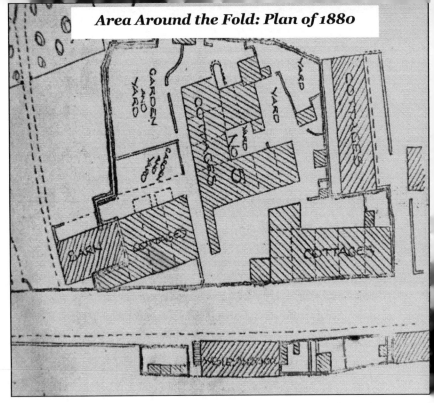

Area Around the Fold: Plan of 1880

In 1857 Henry Butterfield, a confectioner, was declared insolvent but the advertisement of 1861 (above) shows that he was back on his feet and trading again from his small confectionery business at number 2 Holt Square. Other wholesale confectioners in Higherford were; **1861:** Sam Haworth (42) who ran the Spice Shop in the malt kiln buildings; William Nutter (22); **1871:** William Sagar (22); Leeming Hartley (12); Benjamin Ashworth (12); John Walshaw (14); Richard Dunderdale (32); Edward Huffindale (21); Hartley Butterfield (45); William Butterfield (18); Charles Sagar (20); Daniel Nutter (28); Robert Leeming (12); **1881:** Richard Nutter (30); William Butterfield; James Smith (38); Mark Hancock (22); Daniel Nutter (39).

Another Village Tragedy

At the end of October each year the young men of Barrowford practised the ancient custom of Mischief Night. This was the one night of the year in which they had licence to wander the neighbourhood and commit minor acts of vandalism. Gangs of lads would congregate on the far borders of the district, usually at the Moorcock Inn, on the moor between Yorkshire and Lancashire, and they would then walk the two miles to Newbridge carrying out as many acts of minor vandalism as possible.

Handcarts were a favourite source of amusement; they would be loaded up at Blacko with all manner of items from people's gardens and sheds and then allowed to run down the hill into the river far below. Gates would be taken from their hinges and carried a long distance before being abandoned. Windows were smeared with treacle and flour and door knobs were tied together with strong twine along a whole row of houses so that the occupants could not open them in the morning. Eventually the lads would return to their homes leaving the village strewn with the evidence of their night's efforts. The villagers would quietly set about clearing up in the morning and cartloads of gates, flower pots and even dismantled garden sheds were returned to their owners in the outlying areas.

In the year of 1896, however, the Mischief Night celebrations were to be marred by sadness, and not, as might be expected, because some daft youngster had injured himself while engaged in a prank.

On the run-up to Mischief Night it had been the practice of local confectioners to make special toffee and sweets for sale to the village youngsters. There were three confectionery manufacturers in Barrowford at this time and all of them made good quality produce. This year, however, many of the corner shops had taken stocks of a sweet called 'Hanky Panky' from a supplier from outside the district. These sweets were bright-green in colour and an added chemical caused them to fizz violently on the tongue. Word spread amongst the village youngsters and quarter-pound bags of Hanky Panky flew from the sweet shop shelves.

Henry Tatham was a bright young Barrowford lad of eight with a shock of blonde hair and a cheeky grin that won the hearts of everyone he happened to meet. On Saturday morning, the 18th of October, Henry and his pals dashed down to the nearest sweet shop and immediately decided what they were going to exchange their halfpenny spending money for. The new, bright-green Hanky Panky was irresistible at the front of the sweet display and the lads were soon out on the street eagerly grasping an overflowing bag each.

They went under the archway next to butcher Daniel Nutter's shop and, emerging onto the village bowling green, they made themselves comfortable on the river wall. Across the river they could hear the muffled clatter of the looms in the old mill while the people living on the Old Row passed by them on their way to the shops. The lads goaded each other, waiting to see who was going to be the first to try the green stuff, and finally decided to try it together. As soon as they tasted a small quantity their mouths exploded with a strange frothing sensation and their lips were bubbling with green saliva. This was great fun but they had better save some for tomorrow as there would be no more spending brass this week.

The first indication that something was wrong came on the Monday night. Young Henry began to feel ill, he complained of a bad stomach ache and his mother put him to bed suspecting the usual tummy upset. But the lad deteriorated rapidly - in the middle of the night he vomited a green substance about the size of a hen's egg and then fell into a coma.

His distraught father ran down to Doctor Pim's house and raised him from his bed. Throughout the early morning the doctor laboured but he could do nothing to save the youngster – the new dawn over Barrowford found young Henry dead. This was not to be the only case involving Hanky Panky; both the Barrowford physician, Doctor Pim, and Doctor Hungerford, from Nelson, reported that they had seen a number of similar poisoning cases around the Nelson and Barrowford district. Fortunately the other cases were less severe than that of poor Henry Tatham.

Higherford Mill Smithy and Tram Shed

This building stands opposite the West Shed at Higherford Mill and was the smithy for the mill. An original ground plan of the mill shows that the water feed for the mill waterwheel could be diverted at the pentrough head and sent under the mill towards Paradise Street. Here the culvert turned and crossed beneath Gisburn Road to the smithy. At one time a pronounced hump could be seen in the road where the culvert crossed. The Higherford Bridge end of the building was adapted for use as a tram terminus in 1903 and was first used on the 8th of August in that year when tram number 5 was the first to rattle its way from Nelson to Higherford. The lines terminated outside the smithy and occassionally a tram would overrun the buffers in which case the derailed vehicle would have to be dragged by horses back onto the lines. The tram terminus served the travellers of Higherford until 1934 when buses began to ply the route.

The Grimshaws

It is impossible to review the history of Higherford without covering the Grimshaw family – this one-abiding name has dominated the history of the development of not only the whole area of Higherford but also many other villages within the Forest of Pendle. Whilst this is not the place to enter into a convoluted genealogy of the Grimshaws it will be worthwhile, nevertheless, to at least acknowledge the history of the family if the subject of Higherford is to be done any justice whatsoever.

The line of the Grimshaw family, upon which the creation of Higherford would depend, can be seen to have migrated out of the area of Blackburn from the 13th century when one Richard de Grymishagh held possession of a tenement from his father, Walter, in the year 1276. Their journey to Barrowford took the family some 500 years during which time they had steadily acquired land and property. Good marriages bolstered their estates and they were not slow to make their mark on any settlement in which they happened to pitch up.

In the fourteenth century a branch of the family lived at Clayton Hall in the village of Clayton-le-Moors and in 1594 a Richard Grimshaw built the house now known as Hewn Ashlar in the village of Fence; this was to be the beginning of the Pendle Forest branch of the Grimshaws. In the seventeenth century there were Grimshaws at Fence Gate and their offspring became established at Sabden and the nearby village of Higham. Thomas Grimshaw, born in the year 1703, married the daughter of John Holt of Loveclough, a marriage that saw yet more land and property being absorbed into the Grimshaw holdings; from this union was born, in 1738, Nicholas Grimshaw of Heyhouse and Higham. Nicholas married Mary Riley of Simonstone, they settled at Higham and on the 9th March 1765 they had a son Thomas – this is where the real story of many Higherford properties begins. Thomas married Grace, the daughter of Abraham Gibson from Stansfield, near Halifax, and their marital home was to be a house in Higham, built by Thomas supposedly to impress his father-in-law. The house is now the Four Alls Inn where the initials of Thomas and Grace can still be seen above the doorway.

Crowtrees 1915

We now move to Barrowford when two elderly uncles of Grace, by the name of Bulcock, suggested to her that she and Thomas move into their house and look after them; the uncles were childless and this meant that Grace and Thomas were assured of the inheritance of the considerable Bulcock estates. James Bulcock of Barrowford was shown in records of 1776 to 1798 as being a woollen dealer, probably a putter-out who would supply raw materials to local handloom weavers and take back finished cloth before selling it on. The residence of the Bulcocks was the Crowtrees estate on the Foreside above Higherford Mill. Grace built Beanfield House on part of the land of Lane Farm and incorporated the old farmhouse (the barn and farm cottage of which stood at the junction of Gisburn Road and Barnoldswick Road until pulled down for road widening about 1924).

The following text is taken from the work of the late local historian, Doreen Crowther of Beanfield House, to whom anyone who has cause to research the history of our district will, at some time or other, find themselves owing a debt of gratitude:-

In her will of 1838 Grace Grimshaw bequeathed to her sons James and Christopher:

All that cotton mill or factory [Higherford Mill], *an estate called Whittycroft and a capital messuage called Crowtrees* [both of these were mortgaged from William Birdworth to raise the capital to build Higherford Mill], *a messuage farm* [Ridge Farm] *and tenement in the occupation of Ingham Walton and a capitol and newly erected dwelling house called Beanfield House together with the estate belonging called The Lane Farm. A messuage farm and tenement called Hubby Causway* [Higher Causeway] *and the three cottages belonging, ten cottages in Upper Barrowford* [Foreside and Gisburn Road], *four cottages at the higher end of the New Malt Kiln, and other cottages belonging* [162-166 Gisburn Road] *together with the New Malt Kiln on the southerly side of the Gisburn Turnpike Road. The Old Malt Kiln on the northerly side of the road, the messuage, farm and tenement called Ralph Laithe and that called Lower Ridge, as well as some dwelling houses in Colne Lane, Colne.*

Thomas and Grace had 9 children of whom James (the eldest son) was born in 1791 and Thomas was born 1794. Thomas married Mary Bracewell of Coates in Barnoldswick in 1823 but this marriage was short-lived as Thomas died on 15th August 1824 and the course of Barrowford history was changed. His brother James now came to live at Beanfield House and by his will of 14th March 1844 he divided his estate into 15 equal shares, of which his daughter Catherine was to have two.

Mary Grimshaw, eldest daughter of Thomas and Grace, married William Bracewell of Coates and the marriage of one of their three sons produced Anna Bracewell. Anna lived at Whittycroft with her grandmother, Mary Bracewell, and seems to have been a somewhat eccentric character. She was referred to by the local council on occasions as 'being very difficult to deal with' and in 1890 an action was brought against her in the High Court of Chancery by John Strickland, of the Grange, for cutting off his water supply which came from her estate. She was ordered to pay £10 damages and an injunction was brought against her to be perpetually restrained from diverting the said water supply - she died in 1910 at Morecambe.

The Grimshaw estate was then sold off and Higherford as we know it today came into being with houses being built on Gisburn Road and Barnoldswick Road - although the houses at Barleydale had been built first on Crowtrees land in 1909.

Higher Whittycroft Farm

Humphrey Hartley owned Whittycroft before selling the property to Thomas Leach in 1712. James Bulcock purchased the property from Leach in 1720 and the farm was then a part of the estates to be inherited by the Grimshaws. In 1752 James Nutter bought the farm and in 1770 Richard Nutter rebuilt it. By 1788 the farm was in the tenure of John Shackleton of Pasture House and had passed in 1803 to the estate of L Shaw (occupied by Henry Hague). In 1825 the farm, at 22 acres, was mortgaged to Thomas Grimshaw at £1,500 (possibly to help finance the Higherford Mill operation). By 1861 the farm was in the ownership of Mary Bracewell and had extended to 32 acres. In 1909 the property, now 31 acres, was sold at auction by Thomas Booth and was described as having 10 head of cattle, 3 horses, poultry, implements, 700 yards of hay, fog and after-grass.

James, son of Thomas Grimshaw, inherited Crowtrees on the death of his older brother Nicholas in 1856, he married Frances Garde by whom he had three sons and a daughter. One son, Christopher, went to live in New Zealand. Thomas Nicholas became Town Clerk of Wakefield and has descendants there and Charles Edward became an Architect (he moved to London where he married Edith Edna

Palethorpe and had a son Norris and a daughter Phyllis). We have a link here with the present for their mother died in 1885 when the children were young and later Mrs Land told me that she could remember someone coming from Crowtrees to school when she was there to tell the children that their mother had died. Only three years later their father died also. Their aunt, Mrs Thomas Bracewell of Thorneyclough, brought up all the children and the estate of Crowtrees was sold.

Thomas had two other sisters, Grace who married Richard Harper, builder of The Willows at Lothersdale and Brookdell, near Crowtrees. The third son of the original Thomas and Grace was Christopher and he married in 1824 Mary Spencer Swinglehurst, daughter and heiress of John Swinglehurst of Park Hill. Had there been any children of this marriage Barrowford may not have had its park as it was through the death of John Holt (who succeeded to Park Hill and died childless) that the opportunity came to buy this estate. It is worthy of note here that the people of Barrowford themselves raised the money for the purchase of the land so that it would not be charged on the rates. Mary, wife of Christopher, died in 1841 and he built the Grange and went to live there, one of his sisters, Harriet Anne keeping house for him until his death. She then, in 1871, built Thorneyclough and lived there until her death in 1890 when her niece and nephew, Thomas and Elizabeth Bracewell, succeeded her.

The Grange: Built 1841

Following Christopher Grimshaw's death the Grange estate was purchased by Nicholas Strickland of Gisburn. He let the estate which was later purchased by Harold Smith and then by manufacturer John Dixon

Most of the Grimshaw men were very musical and took active part in the choir of Higherford Methodist Church, which the family keenly supported. In the early days instruments accompanied the choir and it is said that Christopher could play every one of them. On his visit to Manchester in his capacity as cotton manufacturer, he always attended the service at the cathedral and write down the tunes of any hymns or anthems which took his fancy, adding parts for the instruments and the choir on his return home. His greatest achievement was to build an organ for the chapel which superseded the instrumentalists on its completion in 1859. William Holt, the brilliant young organist and nephew of Abraham Holt of Barrowford, inaugurated the new instrument, the chapel having been enlarged to accommodate it.

The fourth son, Nicholas, died aged 16 and is buried with his brother Thomas in Colne Parish Church; the three other daughters were Ellen Anne, Betty and Grace. Ellen Anne married Thomas Corlass of Keighley and they lived at Croft House (Lower Whittycroft) after living for a time at Reedyford where Thomas had the Hodge Bank Mill. One of their daughters, Sarah, married Rev. Gough, the very well known Congregational minister of Barrowford. One of their sons, Edward, was the father of Mrs Wiseman who inherited Bank House on the death of her Great Aunt, Grace Grimshaw (daughter of Thomas and Grace) who married Ingham Walton.

Ralph Laithe
A Grimshaw property

Betty, the last daughter, is the subject of a romantic story by Jesse Blakey referring to her elopement. Be that as it may she married William Melville Lomas of The Willows in Lytham, wine merchant. They had two children both of whom died in infancy and Betty herself died in 1866 and is buried at Horbury, co. York.

The Grimshaw family built Higherford Mill, which they ran as two forms, James and Christopher Grimshaw and Grimshaw and Bracewell. They also ran the two Malt Kilns on Higherford Hill, so that almost no corner of Higherford was untouched by their influence and owes to the family an immeasurable debt. [I am greatly indebted for much of the information above to Mrs and the late Mr Hanson of Halstead; and to Mr and Mrs Wiseman for kindly offering to me the loan of their titles deeds and family papers.]

Doreen Crowther

The Malt Kilns

Over the years these were variously used as malting works, flour mills, animal feed works, confectionery manufacturing and an egg packing plant. The building (left) is now used by the Heritage Trust

Dicky Nook – Site of Lane Farm

Lane Farm stood to the left of Dicky Nook and the barn stood on the corner where the people are seated in the photograph. Dicky Stansfield, grandfather of Jonathan who built Blacko Tower, lived in the cottage attached to the barn during the late 1700s and early 1800s and it is supposed that the name of 'Dicky Nook' originates from him. However, it is more likely that the name has its roots in 'dyke' from the boundary dyke that ran from Middleton Laithe to the Dicky Nook *(see Figure:3 later for more on this)*. 'Dyke Nook' (*'the corner of the dyke'*) is a name found in many other districts.

The present Barnoldswick Road was built along an old route from Barrowford which followed through Lower and Higher Whittycroft Farms to Stonedge and up to the Cross Gates (a field at Higher Whittycroft still bears the name *'Gate Field'*). The modern Gisburn Road to Blacko is a much later route. Lane Farm was incorporated into Beanfield House by members of the Grimshaw family during the 19th century and the barn was demolished in 1924 for road widening purposes.

Higherford Mill

The first waves of the Industrial Revolution washed over the township of Barrowford on the 24th January 1783 when Abraham Hargreaves, of Heirs House, signed the purchase deed for the old corn mill at Park Hill. Hargreaves proceeded to convert the buildings into a water powered spinning mill and in his diary he noted that he *'Let Grimshaw in* [to the mill]'. This was possibly a reference to Thomas Grimshaw who married Grace Gibson and inherited the Barrowford Crowtrees estate when her last surviving Bulcock uncle died in 1805.

As a maltster Thomas would have had connections with the former corn milling operation but it is more probable that his connection with Abraham Hargreaves was related to the new water spinning venture. Thomas Grimshaw, then, could well have learned the spinning trade by assisting Abraham Hargreaves in the 'Old Mill on the Park.'[1]

Following the inheritance of the Bulcock lands and properties Thomas kept himself busy with his malting business and the day-to-day management of the estate. He was also involved with a relative,

---

[1] For details on Barrowford Old Mill see *Central Barrowford* (Number Two in this Series).

William Bracewell, in Coates Mill at Barnoldswick – in 1822 Baines Gazeteer lists Grimshaw and Bracewell as Cotton Spinning Manufacturers. Thomas was a Trustee of the Turnpike Trust as he foresaw the huge benefits that a new road would bring to Higherford. The new road opened in 1807 in the wake of the coming of the Leeds Liverpool canal to Barrowford and, from a business perspective, Thomas never looked back.

Thomas and Grace mortgaged some of their properties and in 1824 the money was used to finance the erection of a four-storey spinning mill, with a cellar, on the site of the present Higherford Mill. Thomas and Grace's sons, Christopher and James, were set up in a separate business in the mill while the other part was run by the established firm of Grimshaw and Bracewell. The new mill was powered by a water wheel housed in a structure built on to the eastern gable of the mill building. Thought to have been 24 feet in diameter and 8 feet in width the wheel was supplied by water from a 1 acre balancing reservoir.

To supply an adequate fall of water it was necessary for the caul, or weir, to be sited at the furthest extent of the Grimshaw's Crowtrees estate half a mile upstream from the mill.

The Mill Caul: 1910

This was located on the edge of Grimshaw land which ran from here up to the Colne boundary beyond Ralph Laithe. The structure was rebuilt on several occasions following floods, notably in 1837, 1881 and 1967 – it was never repaired following the latter.

In 1832 the mill was fitted with a beam engine housed in a new extension to the western side of the mill. The steam conversion ran in tandem with the water wheel and the chimney was situated high on the embankment to the rear of the mill. The square-section chimney, built in 1832 by Howarth Wateras of Wheatley Lane and Henry Holt, was connected to the Lancashire boiler by means of an underground flue. The reason for the elevated position of the chimney was to enable an adequate structural height so as to create ample draught at the boiler. If the chimney were to have been incorporated into the boiler house, as was usually the case, it would have required a much higher structure and therefore, been much more expensive to build and maintain.

A weaving shed was added to the mill core, on the Paradise Street side, in 1832 but a major fire is thought to have occurred in 1844 which destroyed this along with the original mill building.[2] The wheel house and wheel survived the proposed fire as did the engine house, cellar and chimney and the opportunity was taken to rebuild the mill on a weaving pattern that incorporated more light and so the three-storey building that we see today rose from the ashes.

The new building of 1844 was erected to the east of the original mill and incorporated the surviving gable wall so that the former outside face of watershot construction is now on the inside of the present building. The former eastern gable of the wheel house was removed and a new weaving shed added with its frontage along Foreside. The building of the new shed involved the demolition of an old blacksmiths shop and half of one of three cottages on the site. The owner of the remaining cottages refused to sell the properties and so the new shed did not form a complete rectangle. The half of the incorporated cottage was adapted into the new shed building as a store room and the builders placed iron pillars in the perimeter wall in readiness to extend the shed when permission to demolish the cottages was finally obtained – this never happened and the cottages remain today.

---

[2] Other sources are of the opinion that the original building survived until around 1880. The 1824 building appears on an estate map of 1847 but the surveyor could have simply re-used earlier plans.

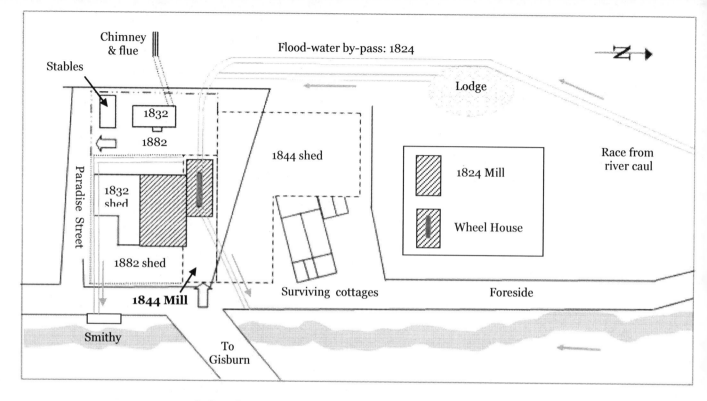

Higherford Mill: Plan showing main building phases

The Hull Packet of May 9th 1826 reported that; '*On the eve of Monday 1st of May at 10pm a company of 200 rioters broke the power looms at the factory of Messrs Grimshaw and Bracewell in Barrowford. They did not force their way into the factory as they had told the owners of their intentions and the owners allowed them free access.*

They then proceeded to Newbridge to the residence of Mr Bolton (of Bolton's Mill) and destroyed 2 looms in an outbuilding near his house. They afterwards dispersed without doing any further mischief.'

Poster: 1835

Someone obviously held a grudge against James Grimshaw. It might be significant that his windows were smashed only a couple of years following the installation of steam at Higherford Mill, along with the attendant move to power weaving looms in the new shed. The handloom weaving habit died hard in Barrowford!

Thomas Grimshaw senior died in 1842 and left the mill to his wife who died shortly afterwards leaving the mill to sons James and Christopher. In 1858 Christopher ran the mill in partnership with his nephew, Thomas Grimshaw, and following Christopher's death in 1865 Thomas went into partnership with his brother-in-law, Richard Harper. By 1868 Harper was running the spinning business alone while Thomas ran 200 looms in the North Shed. Thomas ceased to trade in 1869-70 and the mill was leased on a room and power basis to various small manufacturers. The advertisement for the new lease ran; *'To let - Higherford Mill with immediate possession. Four storey premises with attic calculated to hold 10,000 spindles and power loom weaving shed capable of holding 240 looms. There are about 4,000 throstle spindles (nearly new) with preparation and 150*

VIOLENT Outrage!

About a quarter past ONE o'clock on Saturday Morning, last, the 10th Inst. two front Windows on the ground floor in the House of Mr. James Grimshaw, of Beanfield, near Barrowford, were violently and simultaneously attacked by two persons, who appear to have used for the purpose two large stones of 10 or 12 lbs. each, with which *at only one blow,* they broke 9 large panes of glass, and destroyed the Woodwork of a considerable part of each Window.

The print of his shoe left by one of the aggressors is about 10 inches long.

Whoever will give such information to Mr. Grimshaw, or to the Constable of Barrowford, or to Mr. Bolton, of Colne, as may lead to the apprehension and punishment of the above offenders, or either of them, or of any person or persons who may have aided, abetted, counselled or procured the commission of the offence, (such persons so aiding, abetting &c. *being liable to the same punishment as the principals,*) will receive a Reward of TEN POUNDS; and any information whatever on the subject, will be thankfully and confidentially received.

OCTR. 1835.

looms (mostly nearly new) which may be taken at valuation. The above premises are to be taken together or separately – details may be had of Thomas Grimshaw, the owner. In 1871 the mill was described as holding 200 power looms, 186 of which were made by the Pilling Foundry at Colne – these would have filled the north weaving shed to capacity.

A new business partnership was formed between Thomas Grimshaw and William Holt but this did not thrive as can be seen from a report in the London Daily News of Thursday September 18th 1879; *'Yesterday afternoon (Wednesday 17th September) a riot took place at Barrowford. A number of weavers who worked for Messrs Holt and Grimshaw at Higherford Mill, against which a distress order has been issued, came out armed with fire-irons and broke into the warehouse. These operatives did not get their wages last week and, as a sale is advertised for today, they declared that no goods should leave the premises until they were paid. Two of the rioters were arrested.'*

The Higherford Mill sluice
The sluice gate still remains although the weir was destroyed in the floods of 1967

Thomas Grimshaw (born 1838) died in 1888. John Craven of Keighley ran the mill as a spinning operation from around 1875 until his death in 1879 and during his tenure the mill was extended. Those who do not subscribe to theory that fire destroyed the original mill in 1844 suggest that the new three-storey building that we see today was built within Craven's time at the mill.

In December 1880 Higherford Mill was taken over on lease by Thomas Thornber Smith and Thomas Wiseman (of Bank House). Shortly afterwards Thomas Wiseman took over sole tenancy of the mill (probably on a lease) which, by then, was lagging behind other mills in the area in terms of capacity. Thomas died in June 1882 and his son, Robert Holt Wiseman, took over the business; he extended over his land to the south by adding another weaving shed in 1885 which increased the number of looms to 458. In 1888 a new engine and boiler house was built and in 1889 a new ihp tandem horizontal engine was installed and it is probable that a new iron water wheel of 26 foot diameter replaced the original. This remained until the early part of the 20th century when it was scrapped in favour of a turbine. In 1906 the mill was auctioned by the executors of John Craven and Robert Holt Wiseman purchased it outright for the sum of £4,600. Robert retired around 1920 and the mill was taken over by his sons, Thomas and Robert, as T & R Wiseman Ltd.

Over the following 50 years a series of small manufacturers tenanted the mill including the Higherford Weaving Company Ltd., Hartley Brothers, Ridehalgh Brothers and Rae Shaw & Company. After almost 150 years of textile production the final weaving out process took place in 1971 after which the building was used by various light industrial manufacturers.

The Mill Race

Now disused this culvert carried water from the sluice gate at the river caul across Grimshaw's land to the mill lodge

Grimshaw's Oak

This famous landmark, said to be many centuries old, stands in the Holme on the very edge of Grimshaw's Crowtrees estate. This photograph appears to show a group around the turn of the 19th century – possibly on a church outing

Unfortunately for Robert Wiseman during his first years at the mill the cotton trade entered a protracted period of instability and he found himself having to deal with poor trade and outbreaks of industrial unrest. Following a weaver's strike in 1886 Wiseman agreed an increase in wages of 5% but he reversed this in March of 1888 because of 'local difficulties – this led to another strike of the workforce.

In 1889 the Manchester Times of Saturday 4th May reported that: *'A question was asked on Thursday (2nd May) of the Home Secretary in the House of Commons if he was aware of the breach of factory regulations on the 5th April. The Burnley district factory inspector had visited Higherford Mill and found that the employers were deducting 1s 2d per week from the wages of weavers towards the expenses of employing a man to oil the looms. This was contrary to the Truck Act. The Home Secretary replied that the subject of deductions had been covered in the law courts and the law is not perfectly clear about it.'*

In the summer of 1893 industrial relations at the mill plummeted. Trade was bad and Wiseman was now trading within the partnership of Smith and Wiseman. The workforce were unhappy that some local mill owners refused to pay parity with weavers in other districts but Wiseman stated that his mill was at a disadvantage owing to the distance that coal had to be carried to Higherford. This meant that fuel for the boilers was costing more than the mills nearer to the Nelson railway station and therefore wages had to be kept down in order for Higherford to compete. This did not impress the workers and one of the longest strikes in the history of local textile production ensued. Finally, in the following year, the Birmingham Daily Post of Saturday 16th March 1895 was able to run the following story; *'The weavers who have been on strike for 36 weeks at Higherford Mills have returned to their employment. The loss in wages to the operatives has been over £7,000 whilst the Weavers Association has distributed over £3,000 to the operatives making the total strike costs £10,000.'*

In 1994 the spectre of demolition that has so insidiously visited other fine examples of our heritage was yet again seen to stalk the streets of Barrowford. Higherford Mill was the subject of a planning application that, if successful, would see its demise - a modern estate of twenty four houses would take the place of this grand old building. Thankfully there was to be salvation in the form of the public, individuals and the Heritage Trust for the North West.

The 1st Floor Mill Warehouse in 1994
The poor state of some of the roofing timbers can clearly be seen

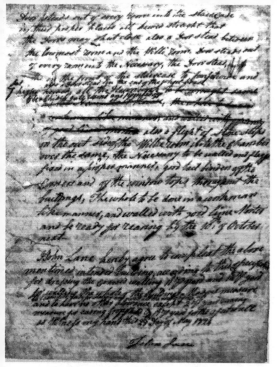

Within five years of the proposed demolition of the site the Heritage Trust had secured funding from the Architectural Heritage Fund and thankfully the mill was given a new lease of life - the building eventually became Spot Listed in 1996. The Heritage Trust is in the advanced stages of converting the interior of the mill into a Centre for Creative Industries.

Original Mill Building Specification: 1824

Builder John Lane submitted his plans and specification for building the original mill on the 28th of May 1824; the new building had to be *'Ready for rearing by the 10th of October next.'* As we have seen, the building was to four-storeys in height with a cellar, or *'willic room'* as it was described (possibly from the Anglo-Saxon root of *willic* meaning running *water/fountain* in reference to the water supply to the wheel). The new mill was to be erected in *'The Croft across from the new bridge end'* with the ground floor walls of 2 feet 6 inches thickness (11 feet in height), the first floor walls at 2 feet 2 inches (11 feet high) and the top two storeys at 2 feet in thickness (9 feet high). The walls to the frontage of the building were to be dressed *'similar to the Malt House,'* the windows were to be 3 feet 9 inches wide and 5 feet high with wallstone heads, the top and bottom to be Marsden Delph stones 6 inches thick.

A staircase was to be built at the south end of the factory in line with the frontage; the stairs were to have a half-pace in every stone and the steps were to be well dressed and of a rise and tread of 10 inches. A building was to be erected at the south end of the factories at two-storeys and a necessary (toilet) was to be built between this building and the staircase.

A wheel house was to be built at the north end of the factory and was to be raised to such a height as was necessary; the walls were to be 2 feet thick but the back wall (as it was to be built against an embankment) was to be 3 feet in thickness. There were to be 1,170 yards of dressed and coarsed walling with 1,470 yards of random walling. The builder was to be entitled to an allowance for fitting the pen-trough for the water wheel at a 2 shillings per yard running measure and 2 shillings per yard for erecting the extra width of the 3 foot wheel house rear wall.

Back Wall of the 1824 Wheel House

Part of the 3 feet thick back wall of the original wheel house still survives in the cellar. The rear gable wall of the later mill is on the extreme left of both photographs, the wheel house wall was only partly demolished when the new mill was built because it was used to support the incoming pen-trough that carried water from the mill race to the wheel.

The photograph (left) is taken from the first floor and shows the wheel house rear wall with the water pen-trough to the right

The Pen-trough Sluice

The sluice gate that controlled the water feed into the water wheel.

The surviving wheel house wall is behind the sluice gate

Mill Stock Record: 1824

This provides a fascinating account of the cloth pieces delivered to the mill by local handloom weavers alongside the business dealings with other mills in the area

Park Hill

It is fair to say that the Park Hill complex provides the earliest site of continuous settlement within Barrowford. That is not to say that there were no other settlements before Park Hill but there is evidence of building here from the 15th century at least. The photograph above is from a postcard date-stamped 1904 and showing the 17th century facade of the building with its two-storey porch dated 1661. Behind the main façade is a surviving rectangular block dating to the later part of the 16th century but also incorporated within the extended site are the remains of construction dating from the 15th century.

To the right of the old building stands a Georgian wing built by the Swinglehursts around 1780 as a gentleman's residence. At this time the Park Hill property was divided into two and the Georgian house became known as Lower Park Hill Farm. The Barrowford UDC purchased the farm in 1923 and the farm land known as Coney Garth, Mill Holme, Walker Holme and Bull Holme was purchased by local manufacturers Samuel Holden and John Dixon for use as a village amenity. The Barrowford public raised a sum of money to purchase part of the former Park Hill land and this was added to that donated by the two business men and the whole formed the site of the park and playing fields. The Council installed their Clerk in the Georgian wing at Park Hill and for many years afterwards it was known as the Clerk's House.

The Clerk's House

One of two 17th century barns survives at Park Hill – one of these was situated just off Colne Road, to the front of the older building but this was demolished to make way for a house. The surviving barn stands in the yard and is thought to date from around 1680. Originally the barn had a pair of large threshing doors but these were made up in the 18th century when a new outshut was added. Around 1760 an extra bay was added to extend the barn. Over the following centuries the barn was altered by a succession of farmers who adapted the building to suit their own needs; the last re-work was completed in 1907.

Park Hill Barn
The rear view shows at least three different building phases

One family name can be said to have been synonymous with Park Hill over the centuries and that is Bannister. This family originated as Lords of the Manor at Bank Hall near Chorley. In 1386 a branch of the family, in the form of Richard Banestre, took over the Manor of Altham and his younger son, John, not being in line for inheritance of his father's land and property, set out to find an estate of his own.

This family of Merclesden were large land owners in the Barrowford, Marsden and Blacko districts and they appear to have been living on the Swinden estate (which adjoins the Park Hill estate at Colne Water) at least in the early twelfth century. Richard Merclesden 'The Forester' inherited the Swinden estate from his great uncle Adam and it then passed through Richard's son, John, whose own son, Henry, had also acquired the 'manor' of Southfield in Great Marsden before his death in 1432. It was from Christopher de Merclesden, a direct descendant of Richard 'The Forester' that John Banestre purchased the estate of Swinden in 1427.

Richard Merclesden (the name later became Marsden) retained the rights over the land and he paid John Banestre a peppercorn rent in the form of a single rose on St. John the Baptist's Day each year.

John died in 1457 and by this time he had acquired some 200 acres of land which extended to Lower Lomeshaye, Great and Little Marsden, Ightenhill and Colne. In 1461 John's second son, Richard Bannister, gained a special dispensation from the church in Rome to marry Joan Walton of Marsden Hall. This was because Richard had fathered several illegitimate children by his new wife's cousin, Joan Parker.

It is probable that the Park Hill would have formed the centralised unit of a 13th century vaccary; these were large areas of former forest land set aside by the De Lacy overlords of Clitheroe as agricultural business operations. Parts of Barrowford and Blacko were adapted into the vaccary system but it is difficult to date the creation of the very first unit here as different areas of the forest were taken into grazing at different periods. References to Barrowford in de Lacy records of 1296 show that Blacko and Barrowford were each let out as single farming units and in the latter *John le Barowforde had the rent of the vaccary which he holds at ten shillings.*' This early cattle rearing farm held forty cows, one bull, five steers, eight heifers, thirteen yearlings and sixteen calves.

Climate, altitude and the thin soils of the Millstone Grit series (within which our area falls) limited the number of cattle that each acre would support. In 1869 the higher townships of Pendle Forest (above 500ft) carried only one cow to between three and four acres. The vaccary of John del Barrowford was around 150ft lower than the higher forest lands but this would not make a difference of more than perhaps one-half of an acre per beast. From this it is possible to suggest that John del Barrowford's vaccary required approximately 200 acres of grazing for the cows, bull, steers and heifers. The yearlings would have required around forty acres of the less-rich herbage of the higher, outlying grazing and furthermore it is likely that the vaccary would have had an area under cultivation for corn and pulses. Given this, then, John del Barrowford might well have had access to around 250 acres, including his rights to the common, woods and waste lands. The actual area of vaccary enclosure would have been less than the total area of land required to sustain the overall stock numbers. It is possible, then, that the Barrowford vaccary was one of the five forest units in existence by 1258.

The vaccaries gave rise to the very characteristic landscape features and settlement forms which can still be recognised in the modern landscape. The centre of a vaccary was essentially a hamlet with several dwellings and associated farm buildings clustered together. The settlement was often in a girdle pattern round the arable area; footpath and bridleway evidence often points to the long-established focal point of the vaccary centre or headquarters. It is possible, then, that if Park Hill were indeed the centre of the first Barrowford vaccary then the satellite farms of Whittycroft, New Park Hill and Ing would have been the sites where booth men (cattle keepers) tended the livestock related to the central Park Hill operation: (New Park Hill is named as such here in order to distinguish it from the other Park Hill farms).

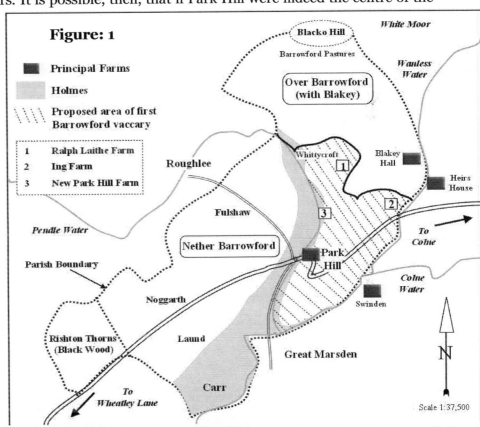

Park Hill lands (proposed) c 1296

The hatched area in **Figure: 1** *represents the higher pasture lands of Rye Bank and the Ing meadows. These elevated level areas would have provided some of the best grass and crop land in the district during the thirteenth century.*

Figure: 1

■ Principal Farms

▨ Holmes

▧ Proposed area of first Barrowford vaccary

1 Ralph Laithe Farm
2 Ing Farm
3 New Park Hill Farm

White Moor
Blacko Hill
Barrowford Pastures
Wanless Water
Over Barrowford (with Blakey)
Roughlee
Whittycroft [1]
Blakey Hall
Heirs House
Fulshaw [3] [2]
Pendle Water
Nether Barrowford
To Colne
Park Hill
Parish Boundary
Colne Water
Noggarth
Swinden
Rishton Thorns (Black Wood)
Laund
Great Marsden
Carr
To Wheatley Lane
N
Scale 1:37,500

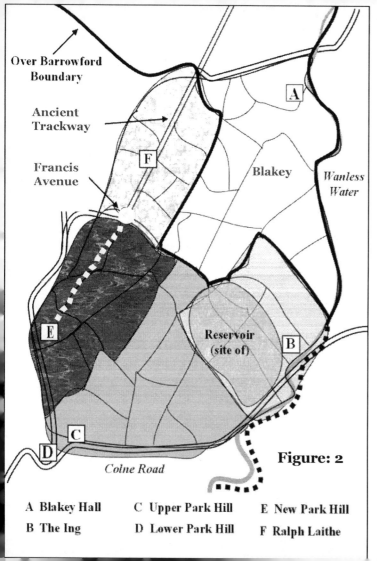

Over Barrowford Boundary

Ancient Trackway

Francis Avenue

Blakey

Wanless Water

F

A

Reservoir (site of)

B

E

C

D

Colne Road

Figure: 2

A	Blakey Hall	C	Upper Park Hill	E	New Park Hill
B	The Ing	D	Lower Park Hill	F	Ralph Laithe

Detail of sub-booths within the proposed Over Barrowford vaccary

A study of aerial photographs, and field boundaries, shows evidence for Park Hill having formed the core of the Over Barrowford vaccary. By looking at the major hedge boundaries that transcend individual fields a pattern emerges where the stages of enclosure can be made out. Further to this 18th and 19th century estate maps show the extent of the land holdings of modern farms and these can often be taken as the areas of sub-booths within the extended area of a core farm.

Figure: 2 shows the field boundary system as it was in 1840 and the old Barrowford/Blacko parish boundary. Much of this field system still remains and aerial photographs, map work and inspection of the extant boundaries on the ground suggest the areas of the four sub-booths which were possibly attached to the Park Hill vaccary operation. The unshaded area was that of Blakey and this covered a larger area than the Blacko township of today. Although these enclosed fields would not have existed when John del Barrowford farmed his vaccary it is likely that the major boundaries that we still see today were in place during his tenure.

Slab Wall and Ditch at Ralph Laithe

Important early boundaries usually took the form of waterways, trackways, hedges and ditches – these latter were sometimes flanked by slab (or boulder) stone walling. Running from the Cross Gates Inn at Blacko is a long disused route down to Higher Wanless Farm; this was once a major trackway from Colne to Gisburn and Clitheroe. A short distance above Higher Wanless Farm a footpath leads to Barrowford off the old track, this point was formerly marked by a standing stone.

The mile length of this path follows in a straight line to Ralph Laithe then along the line of Grange Avenue, through the Grange and across the lawn and down to the 'Old Roman Bridge' where it took up with another ancient route at Crowtrees. Parts of the route can still be made out and the date of its creation is discussed later. The stretch of disused track at Ralph Laithe is particularly well preserved where it is flanked by a ditch and the remnants of an ancient slab stone wall with later drystone infill.

A single field-width to the east of this boundary, and running parallel, we find another linear feature. This is the line of the old Blakey/Barrowford boundary which became the Barrowford/Colne parish boundary. At Ralph Laithe this boundary line formed a 10 feet wide 'headland' (trackway) in the arable fields where the horses and oxen could turn when they had finished ploughing a run in readiness for the next furrow run.

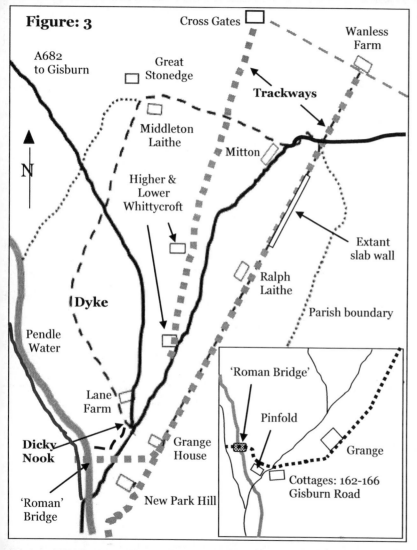

Figure: 3

A682 to Gisburn

Cross Gates

Wanless Farm

Great Stonedge

Trackways

Middleton Laithe

Mitton

N

Higher & Lower Whittycroft

Dyke

Extant slab wall

Ralph Laithe

Parish boundary

Pendle Water

Lane Farm

Dicky Nook

Grange House

'Roman' Bridge

New Park Hill

'Roman Bridge'

Pinfold

Grange

Cottages: 162-166 Gisburn Road

Over Barrowford: Early boundaries and trackways

It was suggested earlier that the name of Dicky Nook could well have originated within the fact that an estate boundary ditch, or dyke, turned at this point thus giving us the meaning of *Dyke Corner*. The evidence to support this argument is shown in Figure: 3 where a boundary dyke runs from Middleton Laithe (Middleton Drive now follows this line) to Dicky Nook where it turned down to the river.

The dyke ran along the back of Lane Farm to the point where the Gisburn and Barnoldswick roads fork, and the 90° turn down to the river at this juncture, would probably have given rise to the area carrying the appellation of *'Nook'*. This boundary can still be followed on early 19th century maps, and on aerial photographs taken in the 1940s, for almost the whole of its circuit around the district of Higher Barrowford. Much of the land enclosed within the ditch and trackway boundaries became the property of the Grimshaws in the 19th century.

162 to 166 Gisburn Road

Following the route of the old trackway from Wanless Farm down into Higherford there is evidence to show that the track ran through New Park Hill Farm to the river where it turned and ran along the south bank (Black Carr) to Park Hill. At a point now occupied by Grange House the trackway appears to have followed across the lawn and down through the former Pinfold to the Old Roman Bridge. This axis can be seen in the angle of the cottages at 162 to 166 Gisburn Road above the old Malt Kiln.

These cottages are built at an angle to the main road and this is possibly in consequence of their having fronted the old trackway. The alignment of the cottages can be seen to follow from the Grange, across the road, along the alignment of the Pinfold, and down to the old bridge. The Pinfold was an enclosure where the stray livestock from a township was held until claimed by the owner upon payment of a fine. The Higherford enclosure covered the area now occupied by the terraced row of Rockville and it is no accident that the Pinfold was placed in a strategic position on what was effectively an important point on the busy highway. Many records exist of local farmers being fined for *'breaking the fold'* at Barrowford where they illegally released their stray stock without paying the fine.

Pinfold

Before the 16th century Higher Barrowford was not well served with trackways other than those connecting the main vaccary farms to their grazing land and a limited number of roads leading to and from the outside world. Three of these latter major routes served our district but the main one in relation to the vaccaries was the Ridgeway which formed part of a very early coast-to-coast trading route. In our area this route ran from the Watermeetings along the high ground to Blackburn and beyond. Along this trackway the vaccary keepers would have taken their 'croin' cattle to Higham to be fattened on the southern pastures there, the better stock would have been driven over to Accrington where the breeding farm was located and, conversely, the chief steward of the vaccaries would bring new stock into Barrowford at the beginning of each new season.

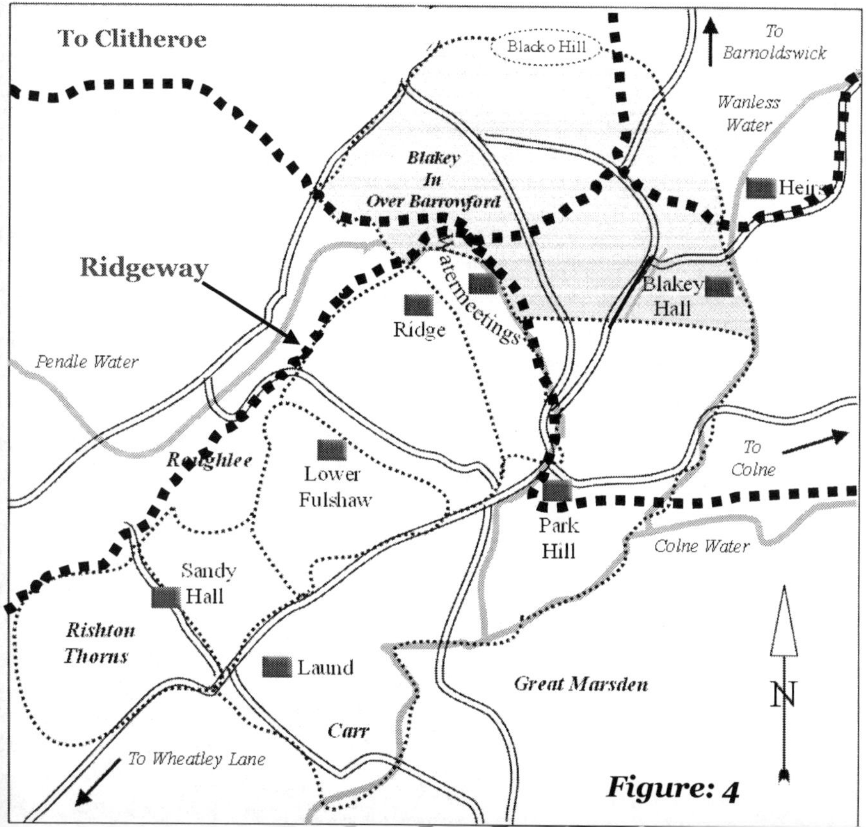

Figure: 4

The Ridgeway

The early vaccary system in Barrowford was served by the three main routes of:
Clitheroe to Colne
Preston to Hull
Colne to Gisburn

Eventually the Ridgeway fell out of use and now has little other use than serving as the Barrowford/Roughlee boundary

The Ridgeway
The ancient route runs R to L in the middle ground terminating at Utherstone Wood

Returning to Park Hill, it was suggested earlier that John del Barrowford would have required access to around 200-250 acres of grazing and arable land in order to support the vaccary stocking levels itemised in the 1295-6 Clitheroe lordship accounts. To locate the first vaccary within Barrowford, then, it is reasonable to assume that the Clitheroe estate would have chosen the best land for the purpose. It is well to remember here that much of the land in Barrowford alternated between the marshy riverside holmes and the rough, peaty scrublands of the hillsides. Although it is probable that small areas around individual farmsteads would have been enclosed and cleared for crop growing and grazing the vast majority of land in the 12th and 13th centuries would range from rough common at best to claggy, scrub-covered wastes. However, it is probable that one area stood out from the rest and that is the raised, level land to the north of Park Hill and to the east of Pendle Water.

This appears to have been enclosed by parallel dykes at a reasonably early stage and, within this area, is a 30 acre field (running from Higher Park Hill Farm to the canal) known as Wheat Field Pasture. The fact that this was a large open field dedicated to the growing of wheat suggests that the land was of better quality than its neighbours and could well have formed the main arable site of any early vaccary here.

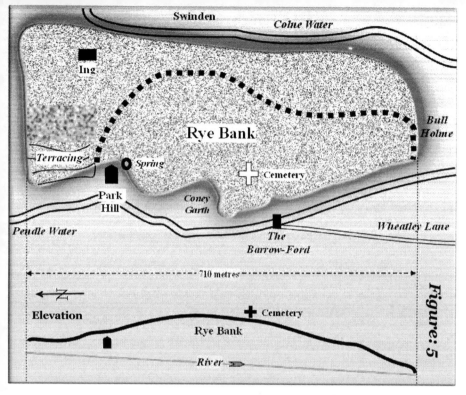

Swinden
Colne Water
Ing
Rye Bank
Bull Holme
Terracing
Spring
Cemetery
Park Hill
Coney Garth
Pendle Water
Wheatley Lane
The Barrow-Ford
─ ─ ─ 710 metres ─ ─ ─
N
Elevation
Rye Bank
Cemetery
River ⇒

Figure: 5

The Park Hill site

In later years the Bannister estate at Park Hill owned the land to the south of Colne Road along which the modern footpath marks a major bank and ditch boundary. This land (Figure:5) remained in the estate until it ceased to be farmed in the early 1920s. If we take this area and add it to the proposed vaccary lands between Colne Road and the Blacko boundary at Middleton then we have a sufficient area to suggest that this might have been John del Barrowford's vaccary based at Park Hill. With his rights to the wastes and woodlands thrown into the equation John would certainly have had access to the 200-250 acres of land required for his livestock levels.

This is not to say that any vaccary based at Park Hill was the first in the area but, whatever the case may be, it is fair to say that John del Barrowford would have been one of the first of many generations to farm the area within the Barrowford parish boundaries for the de Lacy Clitheroe lordship. By 1474 Richard Bannister of Park Hill was the tenant of the vaccary of Over Barrowford which he rented from the King at £4 per year; it might be no coincidence that this translates to an area of 240 acres at the customary rent of 4d per acre. John Walton was the tenant of Nether Barrowford.

John Bannister settled at Park Hill in the 15th century and his son Richard acquired a special Papal dispensation to marry - his son, Robert then took over the Park Hill estate in 1475. In 1535-36 Robert left two farms (Sabden Bank and Stonedge) to his twelve year-old son (or possibly his grandson), Henry, whose guardian was Lawrence Towneley, father of the Lawrence who would later gain the Great Stonedge estate through marriage. Tenants at the Whittycroft and Stonedge farms, at this time were Laurence Wilson, John Smith and Christopher Robinson who, in 1538, were allowed to divide the three estates between themselves. Unfortunately they also fenced off the lane that would become Beverley Road and this led to a heated dispute with their neighbours.

When Henry Bannister came of age he sued Nicholas and Christopher Smith for; *'occupation of lands lying between the Almosse Kyln and Stone Edge.'* The court ordered that each party was to occupy land; *'As set out by mearstakes from the Bryghill upwards.'* The *Almosse Kyln* was an alms kiln for the drying of grain, or for malting; such a kiln stood in a four acre field attached to Great Stonedge adjoining the Blacko boundary – a row of terraced houses was erected on this parcel of land. The *Bryghill* is the sloping land above the 'Roman Bridge' leading up to Whittycroft. This raises an interesting question regarding the siting of the alms kiln; if this is a reference to the kiln at Stonedge then the above law suit does not make much sense. The Kiln Field here adjoins Stonedge and it is difficult to see how the Smiths could have illegally occupied any land between the kiln and the Stonedge land. If this was indeed the site referred to then it seems pointless to stake out the lands from Bridge Hill up to Stonedge as this would not have been in the disputed area.

However, we know that a 'New Malt Kiln' existed on Bridge Hill (as referred to in Grimshaw documents) in the 18th century and it is not unreasonable that this building replaced an earlier one. Records from the 16th century refer to *'The Barrowford Kiln'* and *'The Kiln Yard at Barrowford'* and further to this, the Higherford kiln site is located on the edge of the 30 acre Wheat Field Pasture between Gisburn Road and Colne Road. It would not take a giant leap of faith to recognize that the grain from the Wheat Field would have been dried on site before being ground at the corn mill downstream at Park Hill.

Looking across Wheat Field Pasture
Taken from Spring Grove: the Higherford Mill chimney rises through the trees

The extant malt kilns at Higherford, then, could well stand on the site of the 16th century *'Almosse Kiln.'* In this case the Smiths had pinched part of Bannister's land somewhere along the modern line of the Gisburn and Barnoldswick Roads and this would be the area *'As set out by mearstakes from the Bryghill upwards.'*

When discussing the Stonedge estate as it stood in the 16th and 17th centuries it is worth considering that there was a great deal more land attached than is the case today. At that time the properties that would become Middleton Laithe Farm, Ralph Laithe Farm, Lane Farm and Lower Whittycroft Farm either did not exist or were merely outlying estate buildings. The name of 'laithe' traditionally applied to a field barn set away from the main farm so that crops and animal feed could be stored near to where they would be required. In the 18th century a style of farm building known as the 'laithe house' became popular and these were simply a farmhouse and barn combined in a single structure. However, as far as Middleton Laithe and Ralph Laithe are concerned it is probable that they existed as outbarns for Stonedge. The argument for this can be seen in a Clitheroe Court record dating to May 1564 when Henry Bannister, Gentleman, by a tenant; *'Surrendered a messuage etc. in Higher Barrowforth viz: A messuage in the holding of William Redyhalgh, closes called New Booth and New Ground, in Stoni Edge, and a Barn between them and another called Great Stony Edge to use of Alexander Rushworth and others to be feiffes to the use of said Henry Bannister.'*

Plan for the new estate at Middleton Laithe: 1935
Middeton Drive follows the boundary dyke to Dicky Nook

In this Court record Henry Bannister had gone to the halmote court to surrender a copyhold house (messuage) and land in his over-tenancy to the Lords of the Forest who then re-granted him the tenancy. Bannister then granted the tenancy to Alexander Rushworth (and others) as f*eoffes* which meant that these new tenants would then pay an entry fine to be admitted to the land and property for which they would pay rent to Bannister and his wife on the understanding that these latter retained the overall tenancy. So far so good – we have mention of '*a close called New Booth and New Ground in Stoni Edge, and a Barn between them.*' To show that this barn was Ralph Laithe or Middleton Laithe it might simply be a matter of checking later estate and tithe maps to locate the field names.

Unfortunately many field names mentioned in the records from the 15th and 16th centuries either no longer exist or have been altered almost out of recognition. All is not lost, however, as we find on an estate map of 1847 that on either side of Ralph Laithe are closes of land measuring 2 acres each and both called New Meadow. Therefore we could

MR. J. C. WALTON BARROWFORD.
1/2500 SCALE

well have Bannister's *New Booth* and *New Ground* and Ralph Laithe would be the '*Barn between them.*' The terms New Booth and New Ground signify that this land was taken into cultivation at a relatively late stage within the local agricultural system – probably between 1507 and 1550.

Higher Park Hill

Once part of the Park Hill estate this farmhouse was formerly known as Hilton House. The building replaced an earlier structure which possibly dated to the middle of the 17th century

In the 13th and 14th centuries there was little need for an intricate system of trackways other than the major service routes. The three vaccaries in Barrowford (and Blacko) had cart ways connecting their scattered grazing areas with the main farm, the outlying cattle men's smallholdings and the out barns. These were private tracks for the vaccary with no right of way for outsiders and this meant that the main routes were the only means of access for those who were not connected with the vaccaries.

During the 14th century the Clitheroe Lordship began to relinquish their interests in the estate farms and the vaccaries began to divide into smaller sub-booths. New houses and farms sprang up as waste land was taken into cultivation – a number of 'squatters' built houses on poor land without prior permission but as long as they paid rent to the Clitheroe estate the Lords turned a blind eye. Finally, in 1507, the Forest of Pendle was officially deforested by the Crown and the former vaccary tenants were granted their holdings on a copyhold basis whereby they had a valuable security of tenure. New tenancies were also created at this time and many of the farms that survived into the 20th century were established at this time. The vaccary areas that had formerly covered hundreds of acres, along with the minor gentry estates such as Stonedge, were divided among new tenants – by 1527 the three Barrowford vaccaries had become nineteen separate tenements. Over the following two centuries hundreds of new farmsteads, averaging 30 acres of land each, appeared across the Forest of Pendle.

This was not without its problems, however, as new boundaries and rights of way needed to be established. Where a single vaccary controlled access to large tracts of land the new farms often found that they had limited trackways within their land holdings; their only recourse was to apply to the courts in the hope that they would be granted access across their neighbour's land.

We find such a case in 1549 when Henry Bannister was sued, along with Nicholas Smith and Christopher Robinson, in a *'Suite of Ways.'* The tenants of the farms at Watermeetings, Fulshaw, Higher and Lower Ridge and Crowtrees were demanding that a new road be opened across Bannister's land. In this case the jury ordered that three new rights of way were to be established; one from the Watermeetings to Stonedge and up to Beverley Road; a second from the Alms Kiln to the Cross Gates (probably the *Whiteyate* trackway through Whittycroft) and a third from the Blacko Doles (common land around Cockpit Farm) to Little Stonedge and on to Beverley Road. Today we enjoy what were relatively new rights of way as the countryside footpaths that criss-cross local farm lands.

Higher Laithe Barn at Park Hill
This building stands at the head of Rye Bank on a trackway from Park Hill to Swinden

Medieval Hall
The early Park Hill timber hall would probably have been of such a design

In 1565 Henry Bannister decided to relinquish part of the family's Swinden estate and sold two houses there to John Halstead. The proceeds from this would help towards Henry's expansion plans at Park Hill where he was busy building a stone extension onto the original timber hall and this survives as the earliest visible part of the Park Hill building. Following Henry's death in 1602 his son Robert (who had married Ellen Towneley of Towneley Hall) inherited the estate which, at his death in 1616, consisted of; *'1 capital messuage called Parkehill, and of 3 other messuages in Parkehill and 120 acres of land, 1 corn mill and 1 fulling mill in Parkehill and of 4 messuages and 130 acres of land in Foubrigge (Foulridge) and the sixth part of a corn mill in Foubrigge and six parts of the manor of Foubrigge.'*

Swinden Hall
Now demolished the Hall formed part of an ancient estate

Robert Bannister's 3rd son, Charles (1581-1638) married Ellen Parker of Extwistle Hall and subsequently inherited Park Hill from his father. It is perhaps this Bannister who either created, or took over Charles Farm upon which site the White Bear and Park Shed were erected. Certainly Charles' son John, who inherited in 1637, was borrowing money

from Henry Hargreaves, a wealthy cloth merchant of Watermeetings who probably built the White Bear (then Hargreaves' Great House, or Stoney Hall) around 1667. It is possible that Hargreaves gained the Charles Farm land through default of debt by the Bannisters.

John Bannister added a cross wing to Henry's stone extension at Park Hill which was described in his inventory of 1654 as *'a closet and chamber over a milk house.'* John's will shows that the family was among the top local families in terms of wealth but his death also posed a problem. Where there were a number of offspring, and the family wealth was largely tied up in land and property, it was usual for younger siblings to be left their share in the form of dowries or annual payments for life. This placed a strain on an estate already struggling with poll taxes etc. and the upshot was that families without great wealth or large income streams were forced to remortgage their estates to pay out the beneficiaries. Such was the case with the Bannisters following John's death. John's son Henry inherited these problems and in the early 1660s he was compelled to remortgage the property to John Swinglehurst of Gisburn.

In 1682 Henry found himself having to split the Park Hill estate, half of which went to his son John. However, John was unable to rescue the family fortunes and in 1701 he leased Lower Park Hill to an Ashton followed by another tenant by the name of Gawkroger. In 1706 John took out a further loan of £500 from John Swinglehurst; this was on the understanding that Swinglehurst was to lease Lower Park Hill for 1000 years at a peppercorn rent. The idea here was that John would remain in the remaining part of Park Hill and this might allow him to recover his finances somewhat. Unfortunately this did not come about and John was declared bankrupt in 1710.

The Bannisters managed to stay in their half of Park Hill until 1752 when John Bannister's grandson, John, sold the family's remaining part, along with the estate, to a builder named Yorker. This saw the end of over 300 years of continual occupation by the Bannister family. Yorker sold the estate on to Gamaliel Sutcliffe, of Stoneshey Gate near Heptonstall, and the Sutcliffes, Holts, Swinglehursts, Grimshaws, Hargreaves and Holdens lived at Park Hill until the estate was finally dissolved in the 1920s.

On the hillside behind Park Hill an ancient spring bubbles to the surface before running down to the rear of the old gardens, beneath the old stables and under the bowling green. This would have provided a major source of fresh water for the early settlers at Park Hill. Traditionally this spring was known as *Hell Hole* and the late Fred Bannister, a local historian related to the Park Hill Bannisters, was of the opinion that the village carried this name before Barrowford became the accepted appellation.

Head of the Hell Hole Spring

Looking at the root of the strange name of *Hell Hole* we find the Norse word *hylr* is related to the Old Danish *hyl* and the Norwegian *høl* and they all carry the same meaning of *depression* or *cavern*. *Hel* was a goddess of the Underworld in Norse mythology and the thirteenth century Ynglinga Saga says that *Hel* was the *'howes-warder'* (guardian of the barrow*)*. The close approximation of *Hel* and burial *barrow* is interesting as *hel* is commonly taken to be the Norse word for burial. In either case there is a suggestion that the wooded ridge of Rye Bank, running along the back of the modern day park, was the *barrow* being referred to. Within this extended escarpment are two a sharply defined hollows; the park lake now sits in one and this was known as Coney Garth. Park Hill sits within the other and from here the spring emanates.

Coney Garth in the depths of winter

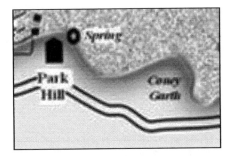

Given these topographical features it is not unreasonable to take the early root of *Hell Hole* as *hel hylr* and thus we have the meaning of '*the barrow depression.*'

Alternatively, given that the spring emanates from a dark hole in the hillside, this might have been considered to have been the entrance to the watery nether world reigned over by the goddess *Hel*. In this case we would see a meaning within *hel hylr* of *Hel's Depression/Hel's Hole – Entrance to the Underworld*. An expert in the Germanic languages, Rudolf Simek, says of the word *hel* that it is; '*probably a very late personification of the underworld Hel . . . the first kennings* (folk knowledge) *using the goddess Hel are found at the end of the 10th and in the 11th centuries.*'

However. . . when the topography of the area around Park Hill is examined it becomes clear that a simpler explanation might be applied. The West Saxon word *heale* has the meaning of *nook* (corner).

With Fondest Love and Greetings from BARROWFORD

In another Saxon word, *halh* (in the northern counties pronounced *hole)* there is a clear description of *hollow.*

It is reasonable to deduce that the name of Hell Hole would originally have applied to the settlement around Park Hill, rather than to the spring alone. The changing language of the post-Conquest era meant that the appellation of Hell Hole was dropped in favour of the Middle English (post-Norman) name of Park Hill.

Having said that, it is clear that the original name survived through being applied to the *'Spring at the Hollow Corner'* in order to differentiate between this water source and others nearby. The fact that local people retained the ancient name into the 20th century is a valuable example of folk-memory in action.

If things had taken a different turn this card would carry the inscription:

'With Fondest Love and Greetings from Hell Hole'

The Park Hill Cruck Barn

The cruck barn at Park Hill is an example of a local 16th century barn. The building originally stood in Cliviger before the Heritage Trust saved it from demolition. The barn was re-erected in Barrowford and, although the stone walls and flag roof are not contemporary with the original, the internal timber cruck-frame has been faithfully restored.

Although the barn is, by necessity, relatively modern on the outside it is well worth inspecting internally.

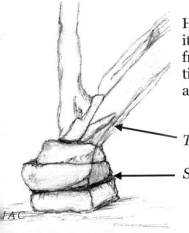

Here we see the original 'A' frame of the timber cruck and the manner in which it projects from stone stylobats at floor level. This method of erecting timber frame buildings has been employed by man since the dawn of time. Placing the timber posts on stone stylobats, or dwarf walls, keeps the foot of the timber away from the ground where it would otherwise soak up water and rot.

Timber posts to support the cruck frame

Stone stylobat

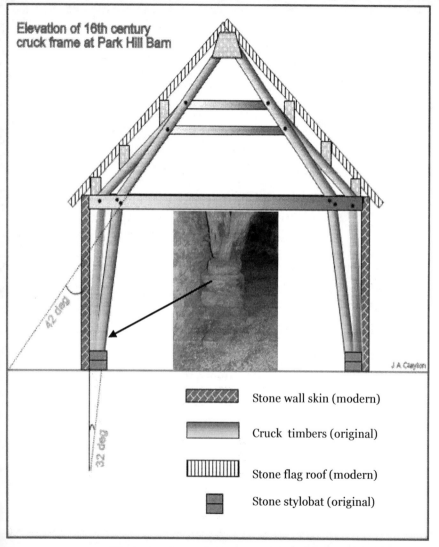

Elevation of 16th century
cruck frame at Park Hill Barn

42 deg

32 deg

J A Clayton

Stone wall skin (modern)

Cruck timbers (original)

Stone flag roof (modern)

Stone stylobat (original)

The Park Hill cruck frame design

The original hall at Park Hill had a similar design whereby stones supported the timber uprights. In a small area to the side of the lane from Park Hill to the cemetery are a group of stones that have been removed from the walled garden area. The example pictured below has all the hallmarks of having been a stylobat and could, therefore, have been a part of an early timber structure at Park Hill.

The 'Old Roman Bridge'

The age of the old bridge at Higherford was much in contention among local historians within the Victorian period. No records appear to exist relating to its construction and Jesse Blakey, in his *Annals of Barrowford*, postulated a date of around the middle of the 16th century.

A Clitheroe Court record dating to 1543 mentions *Brigg Hill*, which runs from the river up towards Whittycroft - this strongly suggests that a bridge of sorts existed here at that time. Whether this was the actual bridge that we see today, or an earlier structure on the site, is open to conjecture but it is not unreasonable assume that the 1543 reference means that the old bridge dates to the early Tudor period.

THE OLD BRIDGE HIGHERFORD

It is possible that a member of the Bannister family at Park Hill erected the bridge to serve his estates and this would probably have replaced a ford that existed hereabouts. The bridge was built without a wall on the top and following a near accident when a cart almost plunged into the river one of the Grimshaw family of the Grange built the walls that we see today in order to prevent further mishap. Jesse Blakey says that a pole was suspended from beneath the centre of the arch with a bell attached to signal any dangerous rise in the river water.

The Old Bridge looking towards Foreside

The wall sides were erected by the Grimshaws in the 19th century

A Deed of Surrender dated 1692 relates to the land in the vicinity of the bridge (this would become the Crowtrees estate) and includes an interesting passage where the bridge is named as the *Oxistan in Barrowford Booth*. In medieval architecture an *oxeye* described a particular style of archway and so we have the meaning in *oxistan* of *stone arch*.

The deed transfers Robert Mitchell's *'moors and mosses'* (at what would become the Crowtrees estate) from R Adington (alias Slater) and John Sutcliffe to the tenancy of George Green of Barrowford. The new tenancy of the *'rood land'* and farm were valued at 2 shillings per annum and appear to have consisted of a farm house, cottage and barn with around 6 acres of land – this was probably the holmes around the Foreside and along Barleydale Road to Robinson's Holme (later to become Grimshaw Holme).

In 1927 the H.M. Office of Works notified the Barrowford UDC that they had scheduled the old bridge as an ancient monument.

Crowtrees estate buildings

For many years this estate probably belonged to the Mitchell family until, sometime around 1700, the Bulcocks arrived (possibly from the Barley branch of the family at Whitehough). Through his wife, Grace Gibson, niece to the Bulcock brothers, Thomas Grimshaw acquired the estate in the later 18th century and upgraded the house (pictured right) around 1805. The barn carried a date stone of 1741; whether this is accurate or not it appears that the Bulcocks were responsible for extending the estate in the earlier 18th century. The property was acquired by Mr Atkinson, who owned the Nelson Brickworks, in 1894.

Crowtrees c 1896

Taken from the track to the Watermeetings this photograph shows an open area now built over. In the distance, between the trees, stands the Bridge Inn and to the right we can see the Crowtrees House and barn. This area became Barleydale in 1915 but prior to this it was known as Robinson's Holme and then Grimshaw Holme. The houses along Foreside and Barleydale were numbered in 1952.

In September 1907 Mr E Hart submitted plans to the Council for the erection of 15 houses on the Crowtrees estate and the development of the area began to spread along towards the Watermeetings. The photograph was taken before 1898 as the Roman Catholic church of S.S. Peter and Pauls was erected at this time and stands directly in the sight line between the old bridge and the Bridge Inn

Rockville
These 5 houses were erected by Hartley Ashworth in the late 1870s when they were known as Rock Villas

Watermeetings Farm (1)

Heading along the riverside track from Crowtrees stands the timber building that was once the Holme Tennis Club. In the 1920s and 30s this also served as a tea shop run by the Sharp family.

A quarter of a mile upstream we come to Watermeetings Farm – a property associated with the Hargreaves family from at least 1609. The building is described by Sarah Pearson in *'The Rural Houses of the Lancashire Pennines'* as a; *Linear three-cell house of two stories, formerly with storeyed outshut at rear. All details suggest third quarter 17th century but final layout results from alterations to earlier build, probably of early 17th century date. The entrance was originally a through-passage. Both west end rooms have corner fireplaces and a blocked doorway to the east of the outshut indicates the presence of a former stairway leading back into the first floor of the house.*

Mentioned in James Hargreaves' will of 1674 is a heated 'shop' – it was common at this time for yeoman's houses to have an attached workshop for the purposes of weaving, wool carding and combing, spinning, cloth finishing and general maintenance to farm equipment. We know that Henry Hargreaves made agreat deal of money from the cloth trade due to records of his money lending activities.

Watermeetings Farm (2)

We saw earlier that the Bannisters of Park Hill were regularly in need of funds during the 17th century and on the 15th July 1652 John Bannister borrowed £200 from Henry Hargreaves, alias Hall, of Watermeetings. Hargreaves is described by Bannister as *'A very hard, oppressing and vigorous man.'* Hargreaves was also described as *'A very rich and able man in estate who set out much money on hire, lending to Bannister at 8%.'*

Although the Watermeetings property is not mentioned in the published Court Rolls of 1425-1567 they do show that in 1527 and 1539 a Lawrence Hargreaves had the second highest rent of anyone in the whole of Lower and Higher Barrowford. It is not clear that Lawrence lived on the Watermeetings site at this time but it seems probable that he did so. The farm and cottage were certainly in existence in the 16th century as there are records of the Hargreaves family being buried at Colne from 1609.

The Poll Tax records of 1660 show Henry Hargreaves who is living with James Hargreaves of Watermeetings. Henry is possibly the illegitimate son of a daughter of James Hargreaves and a Hall, as Christopher Hall, of Watermeetings, had an illegitimate son in 1637.

Watermeetings Farm (3)

On 15th December 1656: Lawrence Hargreaves, a clothier, son of James Hargreaves, married Ann Robinson of Marsden and in 1657 their son John was baptised. Lawrence then moved to Marsden.

Joseph Robinson of Little Marsden, Yeoman, possibly the father of Ann Robinson (wife of Lawrence), is one of the appraisers of the goods and chattels of James Hargreaves on his death. The will of 25th March 1673 shows that he devised (*inter alia*) Watermeetings, a field of 8 acres called Whitelee and 12 acres in Blacko on copyhold rent of £0: 13s: 4d to James, his eldest son and heir. He left his tenements in Barrowford and Salterforth to his youngest son, William. His son, James Hargreaves, was the Executor.

James's belongings were valued by James Hartley of Wanless – John Hartley of Roughlee – John Blakey of Colne – Joseph Robinson of Little Marsden. The rooms in his property were; *The Parlour, The Chambers over the House, The Lower Parlour, The Workshop and The Stairs, The Workshop, The Lower Parlour, The Milkhouse, The Kitchen, The Little Buttery, The House, Barn and other Outbuildings.* James, the eldest son of James Hargreaves, inherited the Watermeetings estate but did not live there; instead he lived in Barrowford and rented the farm out to George Hartley.

Watermeetings and Utherstone

In 1687 James Hargreaves' son John died. Either James or John had built Hargreaves Great House (the White Bear) in Barrowford. In 1667 John mentioned his *'new house'*, and other properties, in his will. However, if the date of the Great House is, in fact, 1667 then it must have been built by his father, James, as John was not born until 1664. This is probably the reason that James was not living at Watermeetings in 1674. John's elder brother James became the owner of The Great House and Heirs House, Colne, and went on to become the father of Abraham Hargreaves who began the cotton spinning operation in the old corn mill at Park Hill. James died in 1791 and his will of 1778 mentions his dwelling house as Hargreaves Great House and his inventory shows his effects are still at Watermeetings Farm.

On his death John Hargreaves left his infant son James, born 1684, in the care of his father James. John also had a son John, born 1685, and a daughter Jennet, born 1686. This son John was later given as living at Laund in Barrowford, it is possible that this property came into John's possession through marriage. The son James had two surviving daughters, Catherine, born 1709, who married her cousin John and later lived at Laund. The other daughter, Jennet, married James Lonsdale of Marsden and they inherited the lower part of Hargreaves Great House.

Heirs House, Colne

Owned by James Hargreaves and his son, Abraham

The 1803 Survey of Barrowford shows that Abraham Hargreaves owned the White Bear (called Charles Farm) and Brew House. He also owned Greenhill Farm, on the right, part-way up Pasture Lane, the farm track past this property was given as *'the occupation road to Higher Ridge and the Watermeetings'*.

Fields attached to Watermeetings Farm were:
Meadow – Parrock – Coppice – Barley Croft – Wood South of the River – Holme of Bridge End – Bowling Green Holme – White Lees – White Lees Top – Rough Ing – Cock Hill – Wood Field – Lowest Dole Field – Middle Dole Field – Highest Dole Field – the latter four contain an occupation road.

Buildings were:
The Farmhouse – The Barn – One Cottage – One Loomshop (in occupation of Aaron Nelson) – One Cottage (in occupation of William Holme).

In the later 19th century Watermeetings Farm, along with the Fleece Inn, Barrowford, was purchased by William Farrington Esquire of Leyland; the farm was occupied by Nicholas Dugdale. Later occupants were the Sharp family.

Pendle and Blacko Waters: c 1920

A short distance upstream from Watermeetings Farm is the spot where the streams traditionally known as Roughlee Water and Blacko Water meet – the *'water meetings'* or *'wattergate'* as the area was known in the 15th century. From here along the journey through Barrowford the combined streams become Pendle Water before meeting with Colne Water at the Bull Holme. Now becoming the Calder this waterway runs along to its juncture with the Ribble.

By the time that Blacko Water (*Black Brook* in the medieval period) reaches the Watermeetings it has been swollen by a number of smaller streams. The waterway begins its life high on White Moor, on the flanks of Weets Hill. It is known here as Sandyford Water until it passes beneath the old moorland road to Gisburn where it becomes Greystone Clough. The stream now passes beneath the A682 between the Moorcock Inn and Greystones Lodge before tumbling down the hillside to meet with another rivulet making its way from Greystone Moor. The two streams then enter the Admergill valley where they become Admergill Water. Near to Admergill Hall a small stream from Wicken Clough adjoins and a half-mile downstream Admergill Water reaches its limit at Smithie Hole (at the bottom of Wheathead Lane). Here the stream of Claudes Clough enters (this is shown on a map dating from 1580 as Twirling Gill) and Admergill Water becomes Blacko Water. It then flows across the ancient ford beneath the 1914 Bridge and through Bell Wood below which the water of Castor Gill tumbles into it (this was Oxegill in 1580). Blacko Water then proceeds across Blacko Foot to meet its appointment with Roughlee Water.

*One of three clapper bridges
along Admergill Water*

Before the age of the motor car the Watermeetings was a very popular place for local people to take their leisure. On summer weekends the riverside walks were crowded with mill workers taking the fresh air and generally enjoying the tranquillity of the place.

There is evidence within the landscape that the Watermeetings was also a very busy site when our ancient forebears walked the earth. At this point it is well to recall that the pre-Roman trade route of the Ridgeway terminated in the Watermeetings valley before it branched out along a number of onward routes. The valley itself is created by the 1,000 foot Blacko Hill which effectively acts as a stopper at the head of the Roughlee and Barrowford valleys and thus provides a sheltered river valley from which travel along the riverways and ridgeways could be controlled.

Where the two streams of the Roughlee and Blacko Waters meet a footpath crosses the White Lees Meadow as it rises sharply up towards the level plateau of White Lees Top. Along the slope of the White Lees can be seen a series of terraces and these indicate one of two things – either they were defensive ditches (ramparts) to control the movement of people through the valley or they were lynchets formed by continuous ploughing of the land. The owner of the land informs me that he has filled in parts of what were deep ditches along these terraces and, along with the fact that there are remains of stone revetments along the edges of the terraces, we have a strong case for a defended site.

Looking up White Lees Meadow across the terrace features

It is interesting to note that the proposed defended site is exactly mid-way between the known Iron Age hillfort at Castercliffe and the Bronze Age hillfort at Middop. It is also at the northern end of the Ridgeway which passes through the hillfort at Portfield near Whalley.

The Watermeetings site is an enclosed area of around 12 hectares within natural ditches and river escarpments formed by Roughlee Water and Blacko Water and the suggestion at this stage is that it was possibly a defended Iron Age settlement within which people could live and keep their livestock safe in times of danger. During the Iron Age the climate became somewhat hostile and the separate tribes were continually raiding the lands and livestock of other tribes people and so it was vital that the farmers within each locality had recourse to a defended site. At the Roughlee end of the site a large mound, surrounded by ditches, sits in the centre of the valley and this could have acted as both a defence against the unwanted movement of people through the valley and also as a defence for the interior of the proposed Watermeetings site enclosure. We are hoping to take part in a formal archaeological survey in the Spring of 2010 in order to verify (or otherwise) the proposal for this having been a pre-Roman site of some importance.

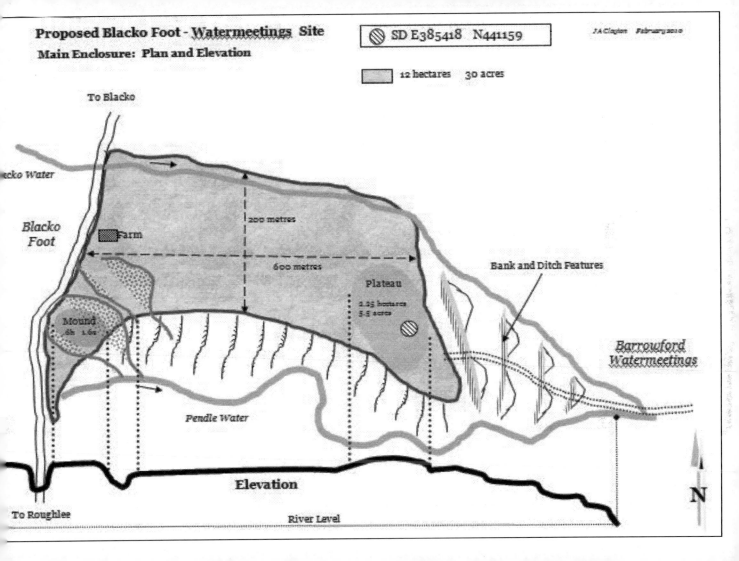

Proposed Blacko Foot - Watermeetings Site
Main Enclosure: Plan and Elevation

SD E385418 N441159

J.A.Clayton February 2010

12 hectares 30 acres

To Blacko

Blacko Water

Blacko Foot

Farm

200 metres

600 metres

Plateau

1.25 hectares
3.5 acres

Bank and Ditch Features

Mound
6h 1.6a

Barrowford Watermeetings

Pendle Water

Elevation

To Roughlee

River Level

N

Ridge Farm

UTHERSTONE HIGHERFORD

The Ridgeway track from the Watermeetings valley ascends through Utherstone Wood, above Higher Ridge Farm and along the Roughlee/Barrowford boundary before crossing the top of Pasture Lane. The slopes of Utherstone were quarried in the 18th and 19th centuries and a number of local structures were built using the stone from here – these include the Higherford Bridge and the Barrowford canal locks.

The name of Utherstone has been variously given in records over the centuries as Huddertstone, Hotherstone and Hunderstone. Perhaps a viable explanation for the root of the name can be found in the Old English (Anglo-Saxon) term of *Hudder* which signifies *'woodsman.'* The appended term of *stone* could well relate to the large blocks of gritstone that rise out of the ground in this area. Further to this a 16th century record refers to a stone circle within this area as the *'Ringstone Hill.'*

There is a record of a local landowner building himself a house in the later 15th century *'Below the Staneshawe Wood and to the east of the Black Brooke.'* This almost certainly related to Utherstone and Blacko Water – the householder was ordered to demolish his property in 1498 as *'It interfered with the Roughlee vaccary there.'* The house would have been located close to the meeting of the two streams of Blacko Water and Roughlee Water.

The Ridgeway between Utherstone and Pasture Lane

On the Ordnance Survey map a row of cottages on the right-hand side, near to the top of Pasture Lane, Barrowford (SD 852 403) is marked as Spittlefield Head. The *Spittle* appellation (sometimes spelt *spital*) is of interest as it was almost always related to their having had some past connection to a hospital of one sort or another. Given the fact that this particular site is known as Spittlefield Head it is not unreasonable to assume that this was the upper limit of the area; taking the Pasture Lane roadway as the southern boundary then the Head is an apt description of the point where the site meets with the ridge-top trackway forming the northern Barrowford boundary with Roughlee. In other words, climbing out of the Barrowford valley the Spittlefield Head is located at the higher point of the extended Spittle Fields.

During the medieval era it was common for wealthy landowners to patronize one of the Hospitaller orders such as the Hospitaller Order of Saint Lazarus of Jerusalem. This was one of the oldest confraternities of chivalry and is believed to have been founded by Saint Basil the Great in the 4th century. The origins of this order go back to the Infirmary of Saint Lazarus, a leper colony established outside the walls of Jerusalem near to the established home of Saint Lazarus. This Order was the only one dedicated specifically to the care of lepers throughout the near east and Europe during the Middle Ages. Lazarites not only ministered to the care of lepers but also to the sufferers of other contagious diseases. The order took on a military role to protect the sick within its care during the Crusades.

Spittlefield Cottages

The Order of Saint John was another Order dedicated to much the same principles as the Order of Saint Lazarus. The dissolution of the Order of the Knights Templar in 1312 resulted in considerable additions to the Hospitaller properties. The king sold off many of the Templar properties so as to settle his own debts; therefore Hospitallers came into conflict with some of the most powerful barons in England. An Act of Parliament of 1324 confirmed the Hospitallers in their rights, but the dispossessed barons entered into a long law suit costing the Order much in expensive litigation.

The four main types of institution were Almshouses; Hospices for wayfarers and pilgrims; Hospitals for the sick and poor and Leper Houses. Not all of these were actually run by religious orders, however; almost 60% of the 12th century institutions were either unrelated to a monastic order or were operated independently from the Mother House. Feudal Lords (often with much prompting from the Sovereign), Guilds and local organisations either ran or supported these institutions. Of these Hospitaller institutions almshouses were the most common, typically being for men only - usually local people who were expected to follow the monastic daily routine. Hospitals catering specifically for the sick or poor were not particularly numerous and by the 15th century many had ceased caring for the sick altogether, possibly because of a decline in charitable funds by the middle 14th century. Because famine and plague had reduced the population at this time patrons were unwilling to support people within institutions when there was a critical shortage of labour.

Height Field (Spittlefield)

Well before the Dissolution of the Monasteries (1536-1539) medieval institutions such as hospitals were in decline - some converted to other uses, such as schools, some charged a fee to the wealthier sick and many others simply disappeared.

Given the fact that the evidence within the Spittlefield name points to a link with one or other of the Hospitaller orders is it reasonable to assume that there would have been a type of hospice on the Pasture Lane site? There is the consideration that the site is somewhat remote at present and in the medieval period was at least two miles from the nearest town of Colne. No nucleated village existed at Barrowford in this period, the area being just a scattered collection of forester's huts, and the odd vaccary farmstead.

It is likely that the area of Spittlefield was within a clustered community, however, as there are early farmsteads along this part of the Ridgeway. Ridge, above the Watermeetings, is mentioned a number of times in the 16th century, as is Ruggall Ing (Ridgaling Farm). Other neighbours include the farms and cottages of Royal Oak, Fulshaw, Lower Fulshaw, West Pasture, Pasture and Lower Ridge. Not all of these were in existence before the 17th and 18th centuries but there is a likelihood that a clustered settlement would have existed here from the 9th and 10th centuries. If a hospital for the treatment of contagious diseases required a high degree of isolation from the main community, whilst still being accessible, then this spot would certainly fit the bill.

Worked stone with possible carving and tenon

The site of the present Spittlefield Cottages once held farm buildings of a much earlier date, possibly of the 16th century. An interesting find in the Height Field, above the cottages, takes the form of a stone measuring approximately 60 cm in length. The stone is around 30cm across and has a form of tenon at one end. On one face a flat area resembling a cartouche has been worked, on this is a single extant piece of carving with the appearance of a stylised eye. When laid on its side it is possible, with imagination, to discern a face within which the carved ellipse forms one eye, the other having worn away. A best guess is that the stone was shaped to fit a mortice within part of a timber framed door, or window, or it could possibly have been a form of stylobat. Another possibility is that this stone was part of the shaft of a cross, the worked end having been slotted into a mortice within a base stone. An ancient stone cross would not have been out of place here if the site held a monastic style institution.

Another interesting stone had been used as part of the wall in a ditch above Spittlefield and this appears to have formed part of the archway of a building – perhaps from above a doorway or window reveal. This was possibly once a part of the farm on the site or, conversely, it might have been part of any structure that stood here before the farm replaced it.

The early leper-houses were eventually abandoned because the disease spread so readily and the Order of Saint Lazarus began to operate larger houses outside of towns; was Spittlefields one of these institutions? Other than the name, evidence for a medieval institution at Spittlefield is scant to say the least. Aerial photographs indicate that the immediate area still retains medieval walling and field boundaries and a disused trackway led from Fulshaw, through the site and down to the old 'Roman Bridge'. The site is located on the formerly important Ridgeway route and levelled areas of the Height Field above the cottages suggest the hand of man - without the benefit of archaeological evidence, however, this is pure speculation.

Medieval archway stone?

Finally, there is the distinct possibility that the name Spittlefield Head refers to an area of land cultivated by the Hospitallers to feed the inmates of an institution in another district. Further to this we have written records relating to the Parker family of Alkincoats in Colne. In the 14th century the overlord of Clitheroe granted 22 acres of land to the Knights Hospitallers of Saint John of Jerusalem within the vill of Alkincoats. This meant that they derived the rental income from the land situated; *'on the east side of Strutwide (OE = paved road) and extended to the pathway going down from the house of Uctred son of Adam de Swinden as far as the brook which was the division between Alkincotes and Colne.'*

This was obviously not the land at Spittlefield Head but here we have the precedent of the Clitheroe lordship donating the use of local lands to the Hospitallers. Although no record of this occurring in Barrowford has come to light the likelihood that Spittlefield Head was land under the control of a medieval institution is more concrete than the suggestion that a hospital stood on the site – for the present at least!

Pasture House

Below Spittlefield Head is the fine Georgian style house of Pasture. The *Annals of Barrowford* says of this building that the architectural ornaments are based on the classical, and are such as were used in the Jacobite period and on a debased style of building in the Georgian period. Some of the walls and beams are very thick (some of the latter being 3 feet in depth.

During the last quarter of the 18th century Pasture was the home of Elizabeth Shackleton who left a series of diaries that have become famous amongst social historians. The diaries run to 39 separate issues covering the period from 1762 until the death of the diarist in 1781. Elizabeth Shackleton was of the wealthy family of Parker whose family seat was Alkincoats Hall, Colne, before the main family settled at Browsholme Hall in Bowland. Elizabeth was born into high society in London in 1726 before leaving the Capital to court her second cousin, Robert Parker of Alkincoats. Elizabeth's father, John Parker, thought that Robert was not of a high enough status to marry his daughter and he refused permission for seven years until finally relenting in 1751. A marriage settlement between Robert and Elizabeth Parker amounted to farms and land around Alkincoats (at £1,000) including;

Alkincoats and closes called the Stuble Hey, Rye Bank, Ingham Field, Ingham Lower Field, 2 little Ings, Hill, Swain Rough Hey, Swaine Stuble Field, Lowest Stuble Field, Spring, Lower and Higher Green Field, Calf Croft, Smalshaw, Jordan Well, Well Ing, Lower Ing, Meadow, Field above Meadow, High

Croft and Hoogate Field; also cottage and closes called the Crosley Fields and Crosley Owne Field (4ac), in Colne. Also 2 closes called Elfylands and Round Inge (7ac), at Colne; also a capital messuage at Holt Edge in Colne and 5 closes called Great and Little Holt Field, 2 Walton Fields and Dencroft (15ac); also a capital messuage in Weddinghall Fold in Lothersdale, co. York. Date 21st September 1751.

Alkincoats Hall

And so Elizabeth moved into Alkincoats Hall with the security afforded by her wealthy family. Robert and Elizabeth had three children (Thomas, John and Robert) in the following few years but her husband Robert died at the age of 38 after just seven years of marriage. This left Elizabeth, aged 30, to raise the three young children on an annuity of £140 per year from her husband's estate. The widowed Elizabeth carried on life as best she could as mistress at the Hall but life as a single woman within a social circle of minor gentry was not the life she aspired to. Perhaps this was reflected in the fact that after a few years of quiet widowhood she took up with a young man named John Shackleton who was 16 years her junior. John was the only son of Christopher Shackleton, a reasonably wealthy clothier of Stonedge who was himself the son of William Shackleton, a merchant from Halifax.

It is likely that Elizabeth's new romance was frowned upon by her family and friends; besides the difference in age, and the fact that Elizabeth had three young children, Shackleton was 'trade' and of a definitely lower social standing than Elizabeth. This was probably the reason why, having decided that she wanted to remarry at the age of 37, the couple eloped to Gretna Green in 1758 where they tied the knot - seven years after the demise of Elizabeth's first husband.

Elizabeth's three children were taken care of through a trust fund set up by their late father but it would appear that some sort of agreement was arranged upon the Shackleton-Parker marriage as, by 1765, John Shackleton's signature began to appear on the children's trust accounts. The terms of the accounts followed the standard procedure whereby the eldest son would inherit the estate property and so Elizabeth' son, Thomas Parker, was in line to take over Alkincoats when he came of age.

In the meantime John Shackleton moved into Alkincoats Hall with his new family and Elizabeth began writing her diaries in 1762. Sometimes she wrote three diaries within a year and the 39 volumes were divided into; *Letters to Friends; Upon Business; Remarkable Occurrences; Daily Occurrences; Memorandums and Accounts.* The entries provide a fascinating and valuable account of the lives of the minor gentry in the later 18th century. Elizabeth ran the house on more of a business footing than a purely domestic undertaking; it is clear that she organised the running of the 14 family rooms, 6 household servant and work rooms and 5 store rooms at the Hall while her husband tended to outside estate matters. In 1762 it was noted that total household expenditure amounted to £292: 0s: 10d while in the following year this had risen to £316: 0s: 6d.

John and Elizabeth Shackleton knew that when her elsdest son reached maturity in 1777 their position at the Hall would be untenable and so, in the earlier part of the 1770s, they began to furnish the property at Pasture House. We saw earlier that John's father, Christopher Shackleton, bought two properties in Barrowford in 1763 – one being the Bridge End Houses (postulated to be the George and Dragon) and the other was possibly Pasture House. Whatever the case, John Shackleton owned Pasture and began to prepare it in readiness for himself and his wife. At this time there are receipts relating to the new furniture purchased by the couple, Elizabeth was entrusted with buying the common-or-garden deal furniture from local shops while John visted the famous Lancaster factory of Messrs. Gillows. Elizabeth recorded one purchase from here as *'A mahogany table in 3 parts – a middle square with 2 half-round ends. All put together making an elegant oval of 16 feet – strongly made and costing £5: 5s: 0d with packaging and delivery at £0: 3s: 6d.'*

Elizabeth Shackleton

A diary entry marked the birthday of eldest son Thomas; *'29*[th] *May 1777: Tom whole and sole master of Alkincoats this day.'* Although Thomas had now reached maturity it appears that Elizabeth had moved into Pasture before this date as she complained that her husband had not wanted to move out of Alkincoats. However, the day before Thomas' birthday he evidently left the Hall for good; *'28*[th] *May 1779; Mr. Shackleton says I stink & wishes he never had me. Two years this day since Mr. Shackleton removed bag & baggage & himself from Alkincoats to come and live at Pasture.'*

Elizabeth refers to her new home of Pasture as *'this cottage'* and here we have an example of the loss of status of which she must have been acutely aware – no longer was she living in a fine hall as the owner of a landed estate. This was not to be her only problem as her diaries make perfectly clear that the marriage was quickly descending into a nightmare for her. Elizabeth had married beneath her status and John had married a woman past her prime and with a brood of young children, one of whom inherited his wife's estate. This did not bode well and the diaries record many instances of John's libertine behaviour – he was relatively young and was not going to give up the high-life easily:

18th January 1772: Mr. Shackleton exceeding rude - threw water on me and vulgar to a degree.
23rd February 1772: Just as we was going to bed at ten precisely Mr. Shackleton arrived here piping drunk from Colne.
8th July 1772: Mr. Shackleton went from here yesterday at noon - staid with his friend the doctor till two this morning, drunk, very drunk indeed.
18th July 1772: Mr. Shackleton threw a hard piece of crust in my face.
7th August 1772: Mr. Shackleton and I quarled at dinner. Porter and beef stakes flew about.

Things did not improve following the move to Barrowford:

6th January 1780: Mr. Shackleton most horribly cross - says he will send for his father to keep me orderly and to comfort him in his great trouble and to rule such an ungovernable-bitch as myself.
15th April 1780: Mr. Shackleton ... is very harsh and cruel with me - I deserve his bad usage.
13th August 1780: Mr. Shackleton gave me a few curses before he went to bed - a happy meeting all night.
1st January 1780: Mr. Shackleton very ill, declares he will lead a more regular sober life.
7th January 1781: Mr. Shackleton came home at 11, as drunk as ever ... the ale he drunk occasioned him to get up and go into the garden.
25th April 1781: The Court Day at Colne - Mr. Shackleton cross and drunk, would not go - Tom was appointed Foreman of the Jury.
22nd May 1781: Dr. Hall (of Manchester) did not apprehend danger in my foot ... my disorder he took to be the scurvy, the gout & the rheumatism mixed ... Mr. Shackleton gave Dr. Hall four guineas.

Elizabeth had complained of ill health for a long period and this appears to have been a result of poor nutrition. It is clear from the diary that both Elizabeth and her husband lived on a diet based largely on meat and strong wine. Fruit and vegetables do not appear to have formed a part of their food intake and this led to them both suffering from gout and scurvy – Elizabeth frequently complained of her teeth falling out and the diary entry for 22nd May 1781 indicates a definite deterioration in her health - the final entry reads: *'26th August 1781: My foot most shocking painful.'* Elizabeth died shortly after she made this last entry and was buried on 2nd September 1781 at the age of 55.

John Shackleton, now a widower, did not hang around for long - on the 5th May 1782 Wilfred Burton, Curate of Barnoldswick, officiated at the marriage of; *John Shackleton of Pasture House in the Chapelry of Colne, gentleman and Mary Cowgill, of Thornton-in-Craven.* John owned property not only in Barrowford but in Colne and the parish of Kildwick. From income derived from these sources he was to provide Mary with an income of £50 per year immediately the marriage was solemnized and he was also to provide her mother, Margaret, with an annual sum of £20 for the remainder of her life. In exchange for this marriage settlement Margaret made over to her future son-in-law the freeholds of Windlefield and Fiddling Clough (in the Earby/Thornton district); *'To hold the same unto and to the use of John Shackleton, his assignees forever.'* At the time of these agreements, Windlefield was described as being in the tenure or occupancy of Margaret Cowgill and John Sunderland, their under tenants or assigns, whilst Fiddling Clough was in the tenure or occupancy of Abraham Foster.

Mary Cowgill had two daughters, Jennet and Mary, when she married John but it seems that the family were to be tragically short-lived. In 1788 John died and left a will:

I, John Shackleton of Pasture House, gent. leave -- messuages called Stone Edge, Upper Lands or Burnt House and New House, and cottages called New Houses, all in Barrowford, with other specified properties there, to Trustees for daughter Jennet. To daughter Mary messuage called Fidling Clough in Thornton, co. York; also £1000. Pasture House, Whitticroft and other specified properties in

Barrowford and Colne, to trustees for my wife Mary for life, then to daughter Jennet, subject to an annuity to my mother-in-law Margaret Cowgill. To my wife a messuage in Thornton called Windle Field, and a messuage in Kildwick, co. York, for life, then to daughter Mary. . . . .

By 1790, however, it would appear that Mary, Jennet and Mary had died as no genuine claimant could be found to inherit John's estate: An advertisement in the London Gazette on Tuesday August 24th, 1790 read:

Heirs at Law wanted:
The Heir or Heirs at Law of Mr. John SHACKLETON, late of Pasture House, near Colne, in the County of Lancaster, Gentleman, lately deceased, as well as of Mrs. Mary SHACKLETON, his Widow, deceased, may, by applying to Mr. Bolton, Attorney, in Colne, in the County of Lancaster, with proper Proofs of their being to receive Information which may tend much to their Advantage. Mr. John SHACKLETON, was the only Child of Mr. Christopher SHACKLETON, late of Stone Edge, near Colne aforesaid, Gentleman, deceased, and Mr. Christopher SHACKLETON was the Son of one William SHACKLETON, who formerly resided in the Neighbourhood of Halifax. Mrs. Mary Shackleton was the only Child of Mr. William COWGILL, formerly of Fielding Clough, near Earby in the Parish of Thornton, in Craven, in the County of York. By Order of Thomas PARKER, Esq.; and Mr. William FOLDS, the Executors and Trustees named in the last Will of the aid of Mr. John SHACKLETON. Colne, August 12, 1790. J. BOLTON.

This advertisement did not elicit the hoped for heirs to the estate but a follow up is recorded when a letter appeared in the newspaper in 1881:

Re: estate of Mr. John Shackleton of Lancashire: R. C of York would be glad if any of your readers can inform her where the estate of this deceased gentleman are situate, the extent of them, and if any heirs have yet been found to the property, which she understands has been in Chancery many years.

A later edition of the newspaper ran the following reply:

Re: John Shackleton, Lancashire:
The estate is called Colne, and is situate in Lancashire. No heirs have yet been discovered who have established their heirship. If R. C (York) will communicate with Miss Shackleton, Tanshelf, Pontefract, she will perhaps be able to supply further particulars.

It is probable that Miss Shackleton, of Tanshelf, was of the extended family of John Shackleton's grandfather, William of Halifax – although she was evidently not a close enough relative to inherit the estate.

In the *Annals of Barrowford* the author, Jesse Blakey, relates that J. W. Swinglehurst, of the Park Hill estate, came into the possession of a diary dating from 1774. The *Annals* relates that the diary was that of Mr. John Shackleton, of Pasture Lane Farm, *'who died unmarried – his considerable estate being in Chancery for many years.'* It would appear, however, that Jesse Blakey did not have the full facts of the Shackleton-Parker family. The diarist is almost certainly Elizabeth's husband, John Shackleton, who followed his wife's example in keeping a diary - the entries are from 1774-75 and relate to the period when he lived at Alkincoats. He refers to Pasture Lane Farm and the other properties purchased by his father; he was renting out the Pasture estate until he and Elizabeth were ready to take up residence there. A number of entries show John's dealings with his wife's son, Thomas Parker, along with other matters of estate:

1774; Wool that my father bought in the country cost £295: 5s: 1d.

1775; Lawrence Ashworth leased the house, dye house and the south end of the garden from me for one year at £8:15s:0d.

James Varley paid by me to build a little house in Barrowford at 7s:3d.

Spent when I went to the White bear to let Mr. Cockshott this farm, £1: 5s, which I did at £190 per year.

Had a few words with Thomas Parker. He told me I was a 'lyer,' com'd of a poor family, had no one that belonged to me, that what I had got it by his mother, which I told him he was a 'lyer,' and that I would not live with him any longer.

Received of Mr. Thomas Parker the sum of £223 which he was indebted to me by the books.

Sold Thomas Tattersall the Holme barn and stable at Barrowford for one year, at £15 per year.

The 39 volumes of Elizabeth Shackleton's diaries were passed down through the parker family and were kept at Browsholme Hall. They were then lodged with the Preston Records Office where they can be viewed; the Local Studies Library at Colne also hold transcripts of the diaries dating from 1764 to 1781.

Pasture Gate Farm
Known locally as the Piece House